A Cornishman
Goes Cruising

George Williams

A Cornishman Goes Cruising

A Cornishman Goes Cruising

CONTENTS

A CORNISHMAN GOES CRUISING

As the band rounded off the last few notes of "We Are Sailing", there was already several metres of water between the ship and the dockside, and the '*MV Oriana*' pushed forwards down Southampton Waters towards the sea.

We simultaneously finished our last mouthfuls of champagne and looked at remnants of streamers fluttering from above and into the muddied waters.

Would the cruise live up to our expectations?
Would I be seasick?
Was it really what we wanted?

This dream holiday of a lifetime took months to plan, but it was really based on a lifetime of my dreams.

A Cornishman Goes Cruising

My Love of the Sea

Like so many other Cornish people I grew up within a handful of miles of the sea. It was a natural part of my life to go to the coast by bus, or pushbike, and later by motorbike and eventually car. The sea was a source of pleasure as something to splash and swim around in with friends. We respected its power because we were continually knocked over by the waves, or dragged off our feet by the rush of water. As we grew older and bigger we succeeded in winning tiny victories against its power by jumping over small waves and diving through larger ones.

The beach was just as important as a place to sit and talk, or to run around playing unexplainable children's games, and then to quickly cool down in the water before sitting down again to rest and dry off in the sun. These cycles of activities helped to speed up the tanning action of the sun, with the ever-present salty breezes resulting in an almost permanent brown skin lasting well into the winter.

In my younger teenage years, the attraction of the sea continued as a major venue to meet friends, and more especially girls. During the summer days it was natural to have informal gatherings on the beaches just meeting up with school friends, or perhaps visitors escaping their parents to seek out the 'locals'. These days usually ended with a smile or a wave, and maybe an unexplained warm glow deep inside the body. Sometimes couples would meet up again for a fleeting

1

romance, rarely consisting of more than short walks away from the main group, perhaps holding hands, and sometimes an experimental touching of confused lips. Although a few seaside romances resulted in lifelong partners, this was rare, as summers were short and somehow as temperatures cooled down, so did our passions.

As the years passed and our innocence was left behind, the visits to the sea were no longer to play those children's games. Our bodies became awkward, and taking clothes off not so inviting even on the hottest days. This left us with white bodies except from the neck upwards, and from the tee-shirt arms down. The groups of friends became smaller, and more activities centred on the evening with barbeques on the beach or dances in the local village halls. All involved alcohol, and most involved the pursuit of girls. Romances now lasted longer and were more intense, resulting in a much higher number of lifelong pairings.

Although I had many pleasant times, leaving me with happy memories forever, I did not meet my wife-to-be until 1974 on a training course in a little Oxfordshire village called Leafield.

I immediately decided to leave Cornwall and work at that training school where the romance blossomed, and we married a year later during the incredibly hot and dry July of 1975.

Like so many Cornishmen before me I then returned home with my new bride, Debbie, and we eventually set up home in the coastal village of Porthleven. We could see the sea from our bedroom window, and felt the power of the wind on that same window for the next 14 years.

My career changed path again in 1989 and I finally left Cornwall, dragging my wife and two children to Oxfordshire where I worked at that same training school again.

I was by then 38, and in all those years I could probably count on the fingers of one hand the number of times I had actually been in a boat on the water.

My home was now landlocked with no sight or quick access to the sea, but my memories remained, and somehow the thought of taking a cruise began to grow in my mind.

Holidays

As a child, holidays with my parents were not far-away adventures, or based on entertainment, but more on visiting relatives and catching up on family news.

When I started work and had the freedom to plan and organise holidays, a major limiting factor was that I was instinctively frightened of flying. Some psychiatrist could no doubt explain this fear but I accepted it, and made a conscious decision to avoid aeroplanes. Hence holidays continued to be spent on the beaches during the day and in the pubs at night.

In fact, the first true holiday I ever had, was with Debbie when we were offered the chance to visit my brother in France. This was also my first trip away from Britain - a chance to experience sights, a lifestyle, and a language that were different to what I had been brought up with. This all fascinated me although the language barrier certainly frightened me. Oh how I wished I had spent more time studying French in school when I discovered with embarrassment, that many French people could converse with me in English, whilst I could not return the gesture.

So I now had a taste for travel, but could not do much about it with my phobia for flying.

The next holiday was my honeymoon, and this was another radical change to my life. After much discussion with Debbie we agreed to have our honeymoon in Weymouth at a Pontins Holiday Centre. I had heard of

4

such places but many of the tales involved their similarity to a prison environment.

How wrong these stories were, compared to that experience!

As well as the excitement and fun of being newly married, the 24-hour entertainment factor of a holiday camp opened my eyes to a different way of spending summer breaks. I revelled in being served by waiters, and entertained by singers and comedians, with young Blue Coated people trying to get me involved. I didn't need much encouragement and took part in anything that made me smile. Perhaps the abundance of alcohol helped, but I did notice that if you took part and made a fool of yourself, others laughed with you, rather than at you, and I was hooked.

Unfortunately these holidays cost more than a newly married couple could afford, so holidays for the next few years returned, in the main, to visiting relatives. Fortunately my parents-in-law (Jim and Jean) were wonderful, and seeing our financial limitations shared some of their holidays with us at small holiday camps.

My ideal holiday criteria were now forming.

It should ideally involve foreign travel without flights, and must include the greatest amount of being pampered, and be inclusive of entertainment.

That dream holiday was a long way off.

Married life became family life in 1980 with the arrival of Andrew, followed in 1983 with Lynsey. By that time my job was becoming more rewarding financially, and we decided to break our holiday trend and return to Pontins. Initially it was an experiment to see if it was possible with a young family, but soon it became apparent that it was ideal for us. The entertainment for adults applied equally to children, and our two happily joined in. An extra bonus was the "Baby Crying" alarm service during the evening, which allowed us to have a reasonable drink together for the first time since the children had been born.

We had some incredibly enjoyable holidays and short weekend breaks around Torbay. In fact we returned to one site so regularly that the manager recognised and greeted us as we arrived. As the children grew we ventured further, and this resulted in three trips to the Isle of Wight on the ferry, and then more adventurous visits to holiday parks in Brittany and Belgium. I had finally managed to achieve the combination of entertainment, service, foreign soils and trips on the sea.

This style of holiday continued until the first hints that Andrew wanted freedom from our apron strings and we had to re-evaluate.

The Caravan Option

In the mid-1990s we moved once again, leaving Oxfordshire to set up home in Stafford. It was now a very long way to the ferry ports of the south coast, resulting in foreign travel being taken off the itinerary again. Holidays now centred on Wales and Blackpool. Whilst Wales was pleasant, I found Blackpool somewhat overpowering because as I was growing older the excesses of drunken and noisy holidaymakers started to make it less appealing.

Whilst in a Welsh caravan park we noticed the abundance of privately owned caravans permanently sited at the parks. This had the potential for holidays at almost any time of the year, with a base to explore the area, and we decided to invest in one.

The caravan we eventually chose was in North Wales on a site with entertainment and close to some beautiful towns and countryside. A few friends and family shared our little retreat when we didn't want it, but mostly it was just for us. There were lengthy stays and weekend breaks, sometimes as a family or just as a couple without the children.

For three years it became both a holiday and place to go and "chill out" from the stress of work. As a family we explored the towns and holiday attractions nearby. As this became less appealing we left the children at the site, and Debbie and I visited Snowden and the villages around it, where life reminded me of Cornwall again with its peace and simplicity.

Eventually its appeal reduced.

We had seen the local sites to the point of boredom. The park's resident band played the same set of songs each evening, and cabaret turns became cheaper each year.

Then a realisation dawned that it was just 12 months away from our silver wedding anniversary, and we really should do something special.

It had to be a trip abroad, but visits to the travel agents brought fear for me because it meant flying. Yet for a while I didn't venture to the shelf where cruise brochures sat because I imagined cruises would be too expensive, and somehow not our thing. But eventually a cruise brochure was plucked from the shelf and glanced at.

With some surprise, the price was not ridiculous for what would be just a *'one off'* special occasion, and the glossy pictures and descriptions actually looked closer to our dreams than we had expected.

Choosing Our Special Holiday

The children were old enough to stay at home and look after themselves, so the decision was made. We would go on a cruise to celebrate 25 years together. But there were now questions to consider.

What cruise line would we choose?

Where would we go?

Ideally we wanted to go at a time that coincided with the anniversary, but eventually we came to a choice based on destination from that first brochure we had picked up.

P&O were the company of our choice, on a cruise to the Eastern end of the Mediterranean on board, what was then, a large ship called *'Oriana'*. It would call at Athens, which appealed to both of us, plus a couple of Greek Islands and two places in Turkey (Istanbul and Kusadesi) as well as a number of other places that did not affect our choice.

One Saturday morning we slipped through the doors of the travel agency, and the adventure began.

Spending approaching £5000 on a holiday was not something I had been used to, and booking a cruise is not as simple as arranging a week at Pontins. The next hour was confusing and slightly traumatic with lots of questions and decisions to be made that we hadn't anticipated.

What grade of cabin do you want?

9

Well that was easy, we chose the best we could afford.

What side of the ship do you want the cabin, and do you want it at the bow end, stern or midship?

We did not know, but by a process of elimination and naïve guesswork chose a port side cabin near the stern on C-deck. This was not at the top where prices restricted us, and also where we were told the ship's motion was more exaggerated. It was not too low down as this meant a lower grade cabin. To be quite honest there were not too many cabins left to choose from, even though we were booking some eight months in advance.

Do you want first or second sitting for dinner, and what size table do you want?

Well that was easier as I suffer from a stomach problem that becomes worse by eating late. First sitting then, and a table for four rather than a large one.

The deposit was paid, and after a return visit to show our passports we sat back and waited.

Had we done the right thing?

Preparation and Anticipation

The next few months were filled with a mixture of concern and excitement. As time went by, the concerns faded because we did a lot of research, and everything pointed to our having made the correct decision.

One of the most successful things we did was to buy a couple of promotional videos from P&O, showing what life was like on a cruise, and more especially some details of *'Oriana'* herself. These videos cost just £6 each, which we had back as credit towards the final payment for the holiday. We still happily look at them today on cold winter evenings.

Of course we didn't believe all we saw, as we accepted that the videos were promotional advertising, and like most such things could only be showing the best bits, and in the best light.

How wrong we were.

The ship seemed enormous, and the idea of sunshine, service, and scenery gradually blew our minds.

The anticipation was broken up by the need to be prepared. Life on a ship meant new clothes were necessary and this was (and still is) alien to both Debbie and myself. There was a dilemma about buying clothes that were suitable for extended periods in hot weather, but which might only be used on a single holiday. Although laundry services were available, we decided to build up a wardrobe that reduced the need for this as far as possible.

11

Another look at the videos and we started to create a list of the sort of clothes needed. It was going to be hot even though the cruise was late in the summer. There were a number of formal evenings where the minimum requirement was a suit for me, and evening dress for Debbie. There was no way we could risk just having a single set of formal wear, especially as we did not want to appear to be 'down market' passengers, compared to other people on board who we believed may come from the other end of the social scale.

Hence the clothing list was started. Multiple changes of underwear, plus tee shirts and shorts were a must. The more difficult area was formal wear for the dinners. Debbie had a few dresses that met the needs and I had a suit, but the idea seemed to be that dressing up meant a greater selection of 'posh frocks'. A dinner jacket for me seemed a necessity, but having seen the prices my wallet heaved a sigh of concern.

Fortunately because we were planning ahead, we had several successes. Firstly we went to clothing shop sales where underwear, summer wear, and formal dresses were obtained at far more realistic prices. The dinner jacket seemed a problem until I discovered that you can buy ex-hire items from the up-market clothes shops that I would normally rarely visit. Having bought the DJ, I suddenly felt very special. Not only was it unusual to have one, but I also felt good when I put it on. A learning point we discovered is that a dinner jacket and formal evening dresses make you the same as everyone else. Millionaires and paupers can all look the same when dressed in a similar way.

Back to the videos again

They highlighted that cruising meant more than a journey. There would be days on the ship in the sun, and also trips to see the scenery and sites where walking appeared to be the common thing. So as well as the standard clothes, we had to be prepared with sun barriers such as wrap-around skirts for Debbie, hats, sunglasses, several changes of footwear and of course sun block.

Another trawl of the shops and the pile of items grew to a minor mountain.

We were now taking a greater interest in the places we were visiting. Decisions had to be made as to where we wanted to spend money and have the organised trips, and where we might just do our own thing. There is a difference of opinion amongst cruising people as to the advantage of organised trips, over savouring the places by taxi or simply staying within walking distance of the ports.

P&O (bless 'em) supplied details of what each destination had to offer, and the organised tours that were available. We were still naïve about many of the places we were visiting, so a strategy of how to make the most of the holiday was formulated.

A tour of Athens was an instant decision, but where else should we treat ourselves to an organized tour?

This is where Debbie came into her own. She is an avid reader, and tourist guides and historical books quickly highlighted that other places on the cruise, had more to offer than we first thought.

13

Debbie pointed out that Kusadesi in Turkey is close to Ephasus, which has some wonderful ancient ruins. Not my cup of tea at the time but it was a holiday for both of us, so that joined the list of must-sees.

Istanbul was similarly endowed with historical sites, and as we were to be there for a day and a half, it would be silly to just wander aimlessly for all that time.

How about Lisbon? That was our first port so we ought to make the most of that as well.

That left us with Santorini (Greek Island), Mytilene (Greek Island), and Gibraltar, which was to be our last port. All three locations were short visits anyway so we decided to do our own thing on the Greek Islands and just use Gibraltar as a final shopping stop.

All these trips added a significant cost to the holiday, but *"What the hell, it was only going to be once"*.

Back to the brochure and videos

How were we going to get to Southampton?

There was a coach service but that seemed a little down-market (incorrect assumption) but if we drove, what would we do with the car?

We were now beginning to realise just how well organised cruises are, as the brochure gave details of parking facilities that appeared simple and secure, but at a price. Alternatively we could travel down on the day before sailing, and stay at a local hotel where they offer free parking for the period of the cruise, but that was quite an expensive service as well.

14

In the end we decided that we would drive down early in the morning and use the secure parking service. This was another chunk of money, but it gave us peace of mind, so that was organised and ticked off the list.

By now we were less than a couple of months from departure and the balance of the cruise cost was paid. The mountain of clothes was growing alongside the extra items such as medicines, first aid kit, cameras (plus tapes and films), guidebooks plus less formal reading material. There were also smaller items such as passports, insurance certificates, and of course jewellery that also increased in volume during this preparation phase. To be quite honest we were getting concerned that it would not fit in the suitcases and leave us room for souvenir purchases along the way. At least we had the benefit of being able to take virtually as many suitcases as we needed, with the size of the car boot being the only limiting factor.

Into the last three weeks and currency for some of the destinations was obtained. We knew that the ship offered an exchange service, but my Cornish shrewdness decided that exchanging currency in a captive situation means high rates of charges.

Then the next magical day arrived when the tickets and luggage labels dropped through the letterbox and onto the mat. It was really happening, and there were just two weeks to go. The majority of the packing was done and labels attached to cases. We planned the final elements of packing for the last evening, and sat back and watched the videos one more time, just in case.

On the final day the jigsaw was completed. The cat was in kennels, various meals were created and left for the children, and emergency contacts plus instructions left as to how to use washing machines etc.

The suitcases were by the door ready for the next morning, and smaller bags with passports, tickets, and money left in prominent positions to avoid a disaster. We went to bed much earlier than usual to enable an early getaway, but I spent a restless night running through endless checks in case we had forgotten anything, and were we leaving early enough to get to Southampton on time?

Our dream holiday was about to begin.

Thursday 17th August - Time to go

The alarm finally went off and put me out of the misery of lying in bed thinking about the next couple of weeks. Debbie and I got up, had a quick breakfast, washed, and completed the last bits of packing. Checklists were scrutinised, bags packed away in the car, maps turned to the appropriate pages, and the final notes for Andrew and Lynsey left in prominent positions to be either read, or probably ignored. This would be the longest time we had ever been away from the children, and getting in contact with us would be difficult, but we believed that everything we could have done, had been done.

Far too early we were in the car and leaving Stafford for the journey to Southampton. It was a dull day, but our excitement made everything brighter. Leaving early was to take account of the expected usual M6 delays, but other drivers must have been warned of our important journey, and the roads were unexpectedly quiet. Onto the M40 and the realisation was dawning that we were much too early. Check in time was nominally 3 o'clock and it looked like we would be there before lunch. We decided to stop for coffee at a service station just before Oxford. This would become a regular stopping point in future years, but of course we didn't know that at the time.

Onwards to the A34 and there was less than a hundred miles to go. Passing quite close to where we used to live the signposts were more familiar, and we were following the same route for some distance that we had taken 25 years before on our honeymoon. The signposts began to show south coast city names, and Southampton was moving up the list of destinations. I had slowed down to almost a relaxing Sunday drive-around-the-countryside speed, but by 11 o'clock some 20 miles short of Southampton, we decided to take another break and have an early lunch. We had no idea if food was available at the cruise terminal so this break seemed essential. Once again this stopping point would be re-visited over the years.

After a leisurely lunch we set off again. Maps were more important now, as this was unknown territory to us, and traffic was significantly heavier as the outskirts of Southampton were reached. We had by now noticed a number of cars displaying the same *'Oriana'* sticker as ourselves, so we were reassured that being early was quite normal.

Could it be that other people were as excited as ourselves?

The final page of the map and instructions were now in use, and Debbie started to scan the horizon to find the landmarks, and maybe even the ship itself.

One of the most memorable moments of the whole holiday was about to occur.

Debbie had managed to locate where the terminal should be and tried to see if the ship was visible. Being an over-cautious driver I was more concerned about the road and other motorists, but what Debbie said next made me ignore caution for just a moment.

"*Wow*"!

I do not remember the actual words, but it was something along these lines.

"I can see a ship over the top of the building but that can't be it surely, it's huge."

"Yes it's our ship; I can see the yellow funnel and the P&O flag."

"Bloody hell it's enormous!"

Having read other people's thoughts about this first moment of seeing a large cruise ship, it is a common expression of surprise, and awe.

Even more common is the same view of seasoned cruisers each time they catch a glimpse of their floating holiday home for the next couple of weeks.

It was, and still is an amazing sight. At that time the P&O ships were totally white except for the yellow funnel, and people all over the world would turn and gaze at them. For some people this was because it was their first sight of perceived luxury, and others just because of fond memories.

Within ten minutes we were parked in a queue system like that used for ferry terminals. Yes we were early, and they had not quite completed offloading the previous passengers, as well as trying to fit in a quick lunch break, before starting to accept the next batch of dreamers.

The Final Waiting

Some 30 minutes later the first of the cars were being waved into the terminal itself, and we were soon pulling up to the directed stopping point. By the time we had got out of the car and opened the boot, a smiling porter was on hand with a trolley to whisk our luggage away, and as it disappeared through a hole in the wall we wondered if it would ever be seen again.

At the same time, the sticker on the window of the car indicating we had booked secure parking was seen, and I was shown to a little booth where I had to take my keys and paperwork. One signature in return for a small packet of information, and my keys were handed over and the car driven (carefully) away to the compound.

Still with a slight look of first-time confusion, a helpful finger pointed us toward the check-in point. There we showed our tickets and passports, received boarding tickets and various bits and pieces, before walking the short distance to a waiting area.

Within less than ten minutes of stopping the car we had our first professional holiday photograph taken against a suitable backdrop, and walked into a large hall that was virtually empty, but which would soon be teeming with excited children and adults alike.

The holiday had begun.

It was already obvious that this was not going to be the same as a visit to relatives, or to a holiday camp.

Quickly we bought a first drink, and telephoned various family members to say that we had arrived. Looking around us we noticed a migration of people to a staircase leading to somewhere that was obviously important or interesting. Not to be outdone, we ventured in the same direction thinking it might just be toilets but in fact it was to the viewing area overlooking the ship itself. Well not strictly overlooking, as it was less than halfway up the structure of the ship, but what a sight it was.

In front of us was *'Oriana'* in all her glory. The viewing gallery spanned from about the bow (pointy end) to about a third of the way towards the stern (blunt end). We could see the windows of the cabins and tried to work out which one was ours. Above us we could just see the upper deck areas with their beautiful wooden rails. Flags waved in the wind, radar dishes swung around, and occasionally someone looked over the side or walked through doors.

But the most amazing sight was below us where forklift trucks offloaded food and drink from lorries and delivered them into the ship itself. The process had been going on for some time already but continued long after we returned to the departure lounge area. There was fruit and vegetables of all kinds, many of which a Cornishman like me had never seen before. There were crates of milk, wine, beer, sugar, flour, frozen mountains of meat and mystery packages of who-knows-what. People were moving in all directions, some in uniform but most in civilian clothes. And yes, there was the luggage going up conveyer belts from multiple section

21

carriages pulled in by small tractors. Maybe we would see our cases again after all.

We made our way back to the seating area. We had seen enough to raise the blood pressure gauge of excitement to critical levels, so some relaxation was required. This was at about 1 o'clock and we knew that there was quite a while to wait yet, so the newspapers came out to pass the time, between regular glimpses at the passengers as they came through the doors. There were young couples, older couples, small and large families. Some were dressed in everyday clothes, others already in summer shorts and tee shirts, but there were also a number of people dressed in what I imagined as traditional cruising attire. The men wore Panama (or similar) hats, blazers, neatly-tailored trousers, the women had bright summer dresses and again hats. Although there were some people who looked mildly scruffy, there was a general effort to look the part.

The hand luggage around us gave clues as to their owners' cabins by showing the deck level. A-deck was at the top where the most expensive cabins were sited. We were two decks below on C- deck, and cabins continued down to F-deck.

We knew that by arriving early we would be boarding the ship earlier, and that time was drawing ever closer. My head was spinning with excitement, and as time passed I gripped my boarding pass more tightly, in case it melted or blew away, so depriving me of my dream.

At Last

"Passengers with yellow boarding tickets numbers 1 to 50 please make your way to the departure gate".

It was time. We gathered our bits and pieces and rushed to the said door. Tickets shown, we moved to the dockside and onwards to the walkway up into the ship. *'Oriana'* was even more enormous from ground level, but all eyes, except for those of the most experienced cruisers, were focused on the entrance into the ship.

As we walked into the reception area one of the uniformed staff politely asked for our cabin numbers, and offered assistance in finding our way to it. We had memorised the route from our numerous looks at the ship layout in the brochure and declined the offer. Although fully prepared, the ship was still a maze of corridors and stairways before we finally found the cabin, with our luggage waiting patiently outside the door.

Ship cabins are not huge, but sufficiently large enough to swing more than the proverbial cat. Our beds were arranged as a twin set up against the window wall with small cabinets between. After a short gap at the end of the beds there was a corner sofa set against the wall of the en suite bathroom, and a desk-come-dressing table on the opposite side of the room. Next to that was a fridge with a television on top which stood against the side of the wardrobe, where there was adequate room to store our clothes. There was even a safe in the wardrobe just large enough to keep jewellery, money and personal documents secure and away from prying eyes. The bathroom consisting of sink, toilet, and shower was opposite the wardrobe with the width of the cabin door between. It was better than we had expected and perfectly adequate.

Our clothes were quickly unpacked and put away, leaving us to read the literature about what was going to happen, plus what to do in terms of entertainment for the first evening. The cabin TV was on when we arrived and played a continuous recording informing us of the emergency instructions, and warning us that we would have to attend a formal drill at 4:15 with our lifebelts. This emergency drill would take place in our 'Muster Station', and that reminded us that this was not a hotel but a ship, that was covered by Maritime Laws and used maritime terms for many places and items that can be alien to new cruisers.

Amongst the various bits and pieces on the dressing table were cabin keys, and little plastic wallets that we could use to carry our 'cruise cards' that acted as identification and the on-board credit system. There was even a small map of the ship that fitted into the wallet, to help us find our way around the ship, so with time to spare we went on a tour of our temporary home.

First Impressions of *'MV Oriana'*

She was vast.

She was beautiful.

In fact *'Oriana'* was overpowering at first with lifts, staircases and rooms of all shapes and sizes. As we worked our way from one end of the ship to the other, we investigated numerous bars and entertainment rooms that were eerily quiet at the moment, giving us the impression that we should not be there. We whispered our comments to each other about each new place we discovered, not knowing how comfortable we would become with each venue as the days progressed.

On the two main decks there were a range of public entertainment venues including the *Theatre Royal*, large enough to sit 700 to 800 people in comfort, a cinema (*Chaplin's*) for maybe 100 people, and two other cabaret rooms known as the *Pacific Lounge* and *Harlequins*. There was a bar (*Anderson's*) that was described as being like a gentlemen's club and certainly gave the impression of being slightly more 'up-market' than some other bars. Elsewhere we found the *Curzon Room*, which was designed for classical recitals or a place to relax in peace. This backed onto the games room (*Crichton's*) next to the library that held more than enough books for everyone to find something suitable for the duration of the cruise.

Linking these decks with others above and below was an atrium with an impressive staircase backed by a huge waterfall. At the bottom of the staircase was the reception area where we boarded, and at the top a further bar and coffee shop (*Tiffany's*) topped by a beautiful domed Tiffany-glass ceiling. Flanking the stairway at the other levels there were shops selling clothes and possible presents as well as daily needs or forgotten bits and pieces.

There were two huge restaurants capable of feeding everyone to a near silver service standard in two sittings. One was called the *Oriental*, and the other *Adriatic*. The *Oriental*, the restaurant that we had been allocated to, was situated at the stern of the ship. Although we could have probably gone in and found our table, we decided to wait until later as the rest of the ship beckoned.

We found a bar known as the *Lords Tavern* that had a more pub-like atmosphere, and this became one of our favourite spots where we relaxed on most days, and enjoyed the regular informal pre-dinner quizzes. At the top of the ship there was the *Crow's Nest* that allowed views over the bow throughout daylight hours or a relaxing drink with music each evening.

Outside on deck there were three swimming pools, more bars, areas for tennis and traditional cruise games, plus a net-encircled court to enable football and a specially adapted form of cricket to be played. When the sun came out, there was more than sufficient deck space to sit or lie in the sun with hundreds of chairs and loungers provided.

What immediately impressed us was the stern of the ship, which has horseshoe-shaped arrangements at each deck level allowing unbelievable views of the sea, plus wonderful photograph opportunities. This probably became our favourite spot on *'Oriana'*, leaving us with many memories of sitting with friends and having a cold beer, or just standing and looking at the sea going by at sunset.

For mild exercise the promenade deck has a walkway going completely around the outside of the ship. Alternatively it provides an ideal place to sit in the shade, or the sun, according to your liking.

These are just a few of the magical places on the ship that we initially found, but later savoured and remembered after we woke up and returned home.

Lifeboat Drill

Cruise ships are like floating hotels, but as I mentioned earlier, they are covered by Maritime laws and safety regulations. One of these is the obligatory instruction in the event of an emergency.

The cabin television and regular announcements warn passengers that they have to be ready to go to their Muster Stations when the ship sounds its emergency signal.

The Muster station is a gathering point close to the lifeboats where people assemble in the event of an emergency.

The emergency signal consists of seven short blasts of the ship's alarms followed by a longer blast. Apart from that first afternoon, this alarm is dreaded by passengers, and probably by the crew as well.

We had readied ourselves for this episode of the holiday by returning to our cabin and locating the lifejackets (in the wardrobe) and of course tried them on well before the allotted time of the drill. The alarm was sounded at the planned time and we made our way to our assigned Muster Station (*Pacific Lounge*), joining an ever-increasing queue of people on the same mission. We were new cruisers, and only realised later that people with experience of cruising, know that it is best to get to the rooms before the alarm, to get a seat near the door.

By the time we had arrived, the room was filling, and the only available seats were near the front. This seemed fine at the time to get a good view of what was happening. The room soon filled to overflowing levels giving an indication of what it might be like in a real emergency. Many of the "new to cruising" passengers had attempted to put on their lifebelts causing even greater lack of space, and also causing amusement, or annoyance, to those who had sailed before.

Eventually the performance started with a quick audio introduction by Captain Richard Fenelowe. His voice had a commanding "booming" sound that gained our attention, but also amused us with his very noticeable pauses, giving the impression that he was trying to remember what to say next.

Bing Bong.

"Good afternoon, this is the.. er.. the.. er ..ah, the Captain speaking"

His announcements during the cruise were always listened to with a smile on our faces, but never ignored.

The introduction was partially about safety, but also a welcome speech to the passengers with the usual *"hope you enjoy the cruise"* items. This was followed by an explanation of what to do in the event of an emergency, complete with a demonstration by the attending crew of how to put the lifejacket on correctly. Various things are explained such as the little whistle that resembles something from a Christmas cracker, and a small light attached to the lifebelt. We were also informed of how

29

to prepare yourself to jump into the water as a last resort. In reality it really is a last resort, as the chances of an untrained person surviving the jump from one of the top decks is probably near zero, and requiring the nerve akin to bungee jumping without the bungee. The session ended with everyone trying on and adjusting their lifebelts with the assistance of crew members. This was another moment of farce demonstrating the lack of dexterity of many passengers.

Now we discovered the reasons for the early arrivals taking seats at the back.

The next event on the ship is 'Sailaway' when most people (new and experienced) make their way to the side of the ship adjacent to the dock. Several hundred people were now attempting to leave the Muster station through just two doors, in order to get back to their cabins and drop off the lifejackets. These same people were then struggling to get onto the open decks to join many other hundreds of people.

This was 'Sailaway'.

It was however, a moment not to be missed, and well worth the struggle.

Sailaway

This moment is a tradition that has been going on for decades, as ships leave port for the start of a journey, or more commonly nowadays a cruise. Debbie and I were lucky, and privileged, to have discovered cruising at a time when this tradition was still very much alive.

By the time we had made our way to the promenade deck, we slipped outside to discover an amazing scene. Most of the spots with a clear view of the spectacle below were taken, and we could hear a band playing on the quayside. Without any further hesitation we grabbed a vacant spot from where we could see the band and the final preparations before we set sail.

As we listened to the seafaring tunes played by the band, we were interrupted by one of the army of waiters offering us a glass of champagne.

...well, why not?

This was the first thing we had bought on board and allowed us to use our cruise cards for the first time. It was a painless experience where the card was viewed and your name and cabin number noted. A few minutes later we were presented with a receipt to sign, plus a copy for our records. Of course this coincided with the completion of the first glass and tempted us to have another.

As we began to get lightheaded from the excitement, and the champagne, it seemed as if every passenger on Oriana was crowding in around us to savour the experience. Of course many were watching from their balconies, and others were high above us looking down from the upper deck. Only the most experienced cruisers, who had seen this so many times before, were somewhere else, perhaps enjoying a peaceful moment in one of the inside bars.

Next, streamers were handed out by the entertainment staff with an almost obligatory *"you must*

31

have one", to ensure the next phase of sailaway was as impressive as possible. We didn't know what was about to happen but were only too glad to join in with the fun.

As the minutes passed, the excitement level grew with laughter and loud chatter from both experienced and new passengers. Discussions between strangers began, and usually started with *"have you cruised before?"* that opened up a chain of possible questions and making initial friendships.

Eventually Captain Fenelowe announced we had completed all the final checks, and were ready to depart. The ship's horn blew a loud rasping farewell to Southampton, and the band moved to the finale tune of "We Are Sailing". Unnoticed by most of the passengers, the mooring ropes had been released from the dock and reeled back into the ship, and water was appearing between us and land.

We were on our way!

The first of the streamers had already fluttered their way over the decks below, and onto the dock, but now the amount of paper increased and the scene was magical, as the side of the ship became entangled with multi-coloured webs of paper. Eventually the dock was too far away to be reached by the streamers and they now fell into the water below.

Friends and relatives had been allowed to watch this spectacle from the viewing gallery where we had stood several hours ago. They shouted and laughed as they waved goodbye to *'Oriana'*. We were new to all this, and we had no one to wave us off, but we quickly caught the spirit of the occasion, and waved back at total strangers as we sipped our second glass of champagne.

The last of the streamers found their temporary resting places, and our thoughts turned to the new feelings of movement, as the huge ship slipped quickly away from the quay and gathered speed. There were moments when Debbie and I stood quietly absorbing the new experience, but more often it was a gabble of excited comments, interspersed with sighs of delight, at the thought of the adventure that was to unfold. We were both apprehensive about what was going to happen, and I certainly admit to wondering if we had made the right decision.

For the next 20 minutes we watched the scene around us as the ship moved down Southampton Water towards the sea. Ships and boats of all sizes and colours passed by and many of their passengers waved and shouted to maintain that magical feeling. The crew had almost completed tidying up the streamers and champagne glasses to prepare the ship for its voyage.

Our First Evening on Board

As we sailed through Southampton Water and wandered back to our cabin, we discovered new places and noticed the different behaviour of new cruisers like ourselves with an aura of confusion about them, compared to those with experience who seemed to walk at a quicker pace, or were already seated firmly on a bar stool.

It was all new and exciting and mind boggling, and a question continued to buzz around my mind...

"Was I dreaming?"

It was time to consider eating our first meal on board. But in the meantime we needed to finish sorting the cabin to best suit our needs for the next 17 days. Then there was just time for a shower, and dress for dinner.

Dining on the ship varied in terms of dress code. There were 'Smart Casual' nights when clothing requirements weren't strict but had to be tidy. The next level was 'Semi-Formal' where the gentlemen were expected to wear a jacket and tie, and ladies had dresses that gave a good impression. The highest level was 'Formal' with dinner jackets or tuxedos as the normal attire for men, with a dark suit as a minimum. Ladies were expected to have evening dresses or gowns, with jewellery dangling from wherever possible. Those nights were truly impressive, and continue to be really special moments on a cruise.

The first night on board is normally casual to avoid problems caused by late arrivals of suitcases. But no matter what the dress code is, the eating experience remains constant.

Arriving at the *Oriental Restaurant*, we were greeted by the restaurant manager and escorted to our table. We were seated by an enthusiastic waiter, who then laid out the napkin on our laps. This was quickly followed by his partner pouring us glasses of iced water while we glanced at the menu and waited to see who would be sitting with us. Our table-mates soon arrived and after a few minutes we had introduced ourselves and discovered we were all new to cruising, with similar initial positive thoughts about the ship.

Over the next hour and a bit we were treated to a multiple course meal of a superb standard of presentation, taste and service.

We chatted to our table-mates, and gradually relaxed into the holiday while we sampled the food, and looked around at the stylish decoration. It was impossible not to look at the other diners and imagine that some of them must be millionaires, or famous personalities who were eating alongside this Cornishman and his wife. In reality there were some people of this nature on board but most were just like ourselves and possibly looking at us with the same thoughts.

The meal was rounded off by coffee and chocolates plus a piece of fruit. This was supposed to be the final part of the dinner but most, like ourselves, took it away for those peckish moments later.

As we bid our new friends cheerio, we staggered back to the cabin realising just how much we had eaten, and looked at the programme to decide how to spend the rest of the evening.

Even after this short time on board I already believed that the decision was the right one and the dream looked like it was coming true.

During that first evening there was little formal entertainment available so we simply wandered around and sampled the delights of the different bars. For instance, we discovered that the *Harlequin Lounge* was the place to go and dance, while the *Crow's Nest* was predominantly a place for peaceful conversation with background music. *Anderson's* was most definitely a quiet bar to drink and chat, and the *Lords Tavern* was as close to a pub as could be achieved on a ship.

Out on deck a few other bars stayed open to allow a drink in the fresh air until darkness and the late summer chill forced the passengers inside.

As the evening wore on the layout of *'Oriana'* was beginning to make sense to us, but the journey and excitement of the day were having an effect and an early night beckoned.

The First Day at Sea

We awoke the next morning to the cabin steward bringing us a pot of tea and a packet of biscuits each. These biscuits are a source of pleasure and amusement to all cruisers, as few are eaten immediately but stored away for emergencies.

A glance out of the cabin window quickly confirmed that we were at sea, with nothing more to see than the occasional ship in the distance. We were making our way into the Bay of Biscay and the sea was not calm. It has a reputation much worse than its reality, but our first crossing of the Bay was not kind to me, and over the next few hours my stomach suggested one of my worst fears was coming true.

Having finished our tea and dressed in our best scruffy clothes, we made a decision to go to the buffet breakfast in the *Conservatory* at the top of the ship. Here we found a mouth-watering array of food. As well as the traditional juices, cereals and bacon breakfast, there was fruits to salivate over, plus breads and pastries to tempt even the most careful of eaters to overload plates and trays.

Breakfast at sea is more than eating, as you look out at the unending views of the sea all around, as well as watching other cruisers. Many of them have similar confused looks on their faces at the assortment of food and the scenery surrounding them.

This became our breakfast venue of choice for the complete holiday. When the weather was less than pleasant we ate indoors, but if the sun shone, we moved out onto the deck to savour every possible minute of a climate that we were strangers to.

Breakfast over, there was a short pause in activities until Debs decided to try out the aerobics session. Being on holiday with total strangers, I joined in and amused fellow passengers, with my inability to coordinate alien movements on a ship whose stability was less than still. After a few minutes I realised I needed to sit out that particular form of exercise, and contemplated the ever increasing uncomfortable feeling in my stomach and head.

Initially a brisk walk on the decks in the wind eased the confusion that my balance was producing, but eventually I decided that perhaps more drastic action was required to avoid the paper bags dotted around the ship ready for like-minded stomachs.

The doctor beckoned.

After the order from Debs to see the doctor I rang for details and joined a small but increasing group of people waiting with similar, slightly pale facial colouring to my own. Fifteen minutes and several £s of on board credit later I walked away with a slightly pained backside and a small packet of pills. I was assured that all would be well soon, but that I would become very drowsy, and I should consider having a sleep. The nurse was not joking and a couple of hours later I was comfortably asleep on the bed, and there I stayed for much of the remainder of the day.

During the minutes that I was sinking into unconsciousness Debs and I strolled around the ship, and like so many others stared at the sea. This is a pleasant activity as the sea numbs the brain and helps to relax away the stress of life at home. There is always the added chance of seeing dolphins or whales, but the sound of the waves and the freshness of the air all seems to add together, to make one forget the troubles of work.

Bing Bong.

"This is the officer of the watch. For those of you on the open decks you will be able to see 'Aurora', the latest P&O cruise ship, about a mile off the starboard side on her way back to Southampton."

Not only was she the newest ship, she was also the sister ship to *'Oriana'*, and a spooky moment to see a virtual mirror image of ourselves ploughing through the waves in the other direction. The memory lingered with us longer than we expected, as later in the year we bought further P&O marketing videos, including the one for *'Aurora'*. What we didn't know at the time was that they were filming that video on *'Aurora'* at that exact moment, which includes the view from her of *'Oriana'*, where we were watching. It was only after spotting a date on the ship's newspaper in the video that we realised the coincidence.

Sleep finally overcame my wish to remain vertical, but when I woke up, the stomach-churning had stopped and food seemed appealing again. The pills were used to maintain a stable, if dreamy, condition for the next 24 hours, and in hindsight the cost of the treatment was well worth it. The rest of the holiday passed without any further problems as Nature had decided, that having reminded me of what the sea could do, it would now allow me to enjoy its better side.

I remember very little of the remainder of the day, but there were moments that have stuck in the mind ever since.

The details have faded over the years but that evening offered us the first of the shows in the *Theatre Royal* after dinner. It was one of many shows during the holiday and none disappointed us.

The evening was rounded off with our first attendance at the Syndicate Quiz.

At this point I would like to describe one of those inexplicable coincidences that occur in life. For many years, Deb and I had been involved in competitive swimming as poolside officials. I had just become qualified as a referee, and whilst chatting between races at a swimming gala, I was informed that another referee (Sue) was taking a cruise at about the same time as us. A few races later we discovered that Sue was actually on the same cruise as us. I can only put the coincidence down to the similar thought process of similar people, but these types of mysterious happenings never cease to amaze me.

Anyway, we did not spend a lot of time together during the holiday, but it was decided that we would meet up with Sue and her partner Joe to take part in those late night mind-bogglers. Hence at the appointed time we arrived at *Crichton's*, which is the quiet room for cards and board games where the Syndicate Quiz takes place.

On most nights P&O cruisers can take part in this quiz for teams of up to six people, with questions that rate in the Mastermind level. It is supposed to be fun, but in reality it is a deadly serious 90 minutes of mind searching for a prize of a bottle of champagne (ish). Teams tend to meet up and stay together for the whole cruise, and on future cruises as well, but the four of us were new and needed another couple with similar interests to make up our team.

In that situation the arrangement is to turn up at 10 o'clock and await other couples or groups who need extra team members, and this is where we met Bill and Betty. This couple were established cruisers with a history spanning several ships and the knowledge of what it is like to be new to the experience. They were able to explain many of the finer points of cruising, plus describing some of the ports we were going to visit. Their advice made our holiday even more pleasant, by having a little prior warning of what to do and what happens. They became friends for the duration of the holiday, meeting up with us for an evening drink, and of course the quiz.

The quiz itself was a disaster as although Debs has an expansive knowledge of many things, and Sue, Joe, Bill and Betty were similarly clever through the experience of life, my knowledge is limited, and the seasickness remedy was not helping to sharpen my brain cells. Our team had an average result, but Debs and I realised the

41

level of the questions would mean it would be very difficult to compete with these teams, that appeared to consist of University lecturers, scientists, historians and good old-fashioned boffins.

This did not spoil the experience however, as the friendly chat was interspersed with humorous answers, and assisted by a couple of drinks to forge a team bond which gave us a late night alternative, when nothing else seemed interesting.

As the night drew to an end, we had been given a lot of advice about the port of Lisbon for the next day, and a promise was made to make a team again whenever we came to the quiz.

Back to the cabin, and a late night cup of tea and a quick biscuit from our hidden store in the bedside cupboard, and it was time to go to sleep and dream of what else could happen.

We were still very much in awe of the cruising experience but were just becoming comfortable with the lifestyle, and certainly looking forward to the days ahead.

Day Two Saturday 19th August

"Good Morning Mr and Mrs Williams, here is your tea."

Another day had dawned and the sea was less angry with my stomach. A quick look out of the window confirmed we were still afloat, and to increase the magic, a pod of dolphins were playing just a little way from the ship. We had heard about the joy of the first sight of these creatures but never imagined how special it really is.

The weather was better, but a mist shrouded any distant views to where we knew Portugal was, and where we would be landing just after lunchtime in Lisbon.

We quickly dressed and had breakfast to maintain that pleasant feeling of having eaten just a little too much.

Debs was tempted into the swimming pool for the first time. I watched her lonely efforts, as other passengers stared in disbelief that someone was actually swimming, rather than just paddling. After the swim, aerobics beckoned again, but today I was no longer tempted to amuse people and so just watched.

This just about filled the morning except for coffee, more discoveries about *'Oriana'*, and then finding a suitable spot on the deck to watch the sights as we turned into the River Tagus heading for Lisbon.

On cue, the mist rolled away, the temperature increased, and land was visible on both sides of the ship. Flashbacks of yesterday reminded me that we had gone to a Port Lecture about the city whilst I was drifting in and out of one of my sleepy interludes. As we stood looking over the bow of *'Oriana'*, the lecturer (Betty Skinner) came on the ship's tannoy to announce our imminent arrival, and to point out the different landmarks she had talked about the day before. These included the Belem Tower, the statue of Henry the Navigator, and in the distance the Salazar Bridge.

As we got closer, this bridge (which is now called the 25th April Bridge) filled the horizon, and a noise like a thousand beehives started to become audible as cars and lorries drove over its metal grated construction. To one side of the bridge is a statue of Christ, which is a replica of the one in Rio de Janeiro. It grew bigger as we moved steadily onwards.

Passing under the bridge is amazing, as although there is plenty of clearance above the ship it looks extremely close, especially as the buzzing traffic sounds grow to a crescendo. Lisbon was now becoming a busy city scene and it was only a few minutes away from our arrival. Betty broke off her commentary to get her lunch and we did likewise, to be ready for our first experience of this beautiful city.

44

Lisbon

Lunch completed, we watched the early moments of docking for the first time. The sun was now hot and it felt as if the holiday had really begun. The colours of the buildings were brighter, many of the sounds were new to us, and even the smells were more intense than at home. But there was little time to savour it, as we had to get ready to go ashore.

This was one of the ports where we were having an organised tour along with several hundreds of other enthusiastic passengers from the ship. The organisation required to offload everyone on time to their allotted coaches is a mammoth undertaking, and becomes an experience all of its own.

For those who are naïve to cruising, it is worth digressing for a moment to describe what organised tours are all about.

When a cruise ship with almost 2000 passengers arrives at a port, many of them will decide to take an organised tour to have a guided glimpse of the point of call. These tours are designed to cater for a wide range of tastes. Some are a mixture of coach trip with short (or extended) walks at a number of interesting places, whilst others are more specialised and concentrate on a single stretch of coast, or a town. For the less energetic there are simple sightseeing coach rides, whilst a few target the enthusiasts with cycle rides, or off-road jeep expeditions, and sometimes even offer a chance to see dolphins. The tour durations vary from a couple of hours

45

up to a full day to match passenger preferences and the length of time that the ship will be in port.

Each tour is given a letter to identify it, and then as people book onto them, the tour office decides how many groups of that particular tour will be organised. Hence tour A might have A1, A2, and so on, while the obscure tours could be just a single group. Quite often the number of coaches available at the stopping point dictates the number of tours. Small islands don't have unlimited number of coaches, and larger ports may be catering for more than a single cruise ship on the same day. Booking in advance usually guarantees a place, but many people decide at the last moment based on the port talks on ship. Good cruise lines get the best coaches and local guides, and P&O is near the top of the quality ratings, so the coaches are generally very comfortable. The local guides all speak good English and stops are included to cater for refreshments, shopping, and of course clean toilets.

As this is a moment when P&O are handing their fee-paying customers over to a third party, there is usually a representative from the ship to oversee proceedings. This might be a singer or dancer from the theatre company, or a member of crew, their family, or sometimes a cabaret artist. They ensure no-one gets left behind or becomes ill during the tour, as well as checking that the correct itinerary is covered, and times keep to the plan.

Back to Lisbon

We were booked onto Tour A, which involved a coach trip to the City with a reasonably long guided walk of the Alfama area of Lisbon.

Our initial meeting point was the *Theatre Royal* where we showed our tickets and received a sticker with the appropriate tour and group number. Showing up early meant that we were in the first group and hence had A1 stickers. We were then asked to sit in the area assigned for that group, and await instructions.

As our group reached its capacity for the coach, an announcement instructed us to go ashore.

"Do not forget your cruise card."

This was a regular reminder that the cruise card is an important item of identification. It acts as your security pass for getting back onto the ship, and is recognised by the local authorities in most ports as a temporary alternative to a passport. Many shops also look out for them to offer a supposed discount, or as an excuse to hassle the punters, knowing they are usually relatively easy to extract money from!

Other warnings cover the facts that pickpockets are commonplace at such ports, and as we are British in unusually hot locations, we are also reminded to take drinks, hats, and have a suitable layer of sunscreen on our pale skin.

Our group was hustled through the ship and down the gangplank for our first steps on solid land for a couple of days. By now the sun had decided to greet us with a heat and intensity that I had not known for a long time, and even after the short walk to the coach we welcomed the air-conditioned comfort that greeted us.

The local guide introduced herself and the driver, and then explained briefly what we were going to see and do. As well as the normal families and couples bedecked with cameras and hats there was a single man who somehow looked out of place, and just a little apprehensive. He was the P&O representative, a guest speaker on the cruise who gave talks on the setting up, and consequences of the English Premier Football League. The cruise was actually a themed holiday about football, but at the time of booking we didn't realise this, and it wouldn't have made a difference to our choice anyway.

He was an unforgettable person, tall with a thin stature and almost bald except for an area of lengthy hair at the back. He reminded me of a character from a film which I couldn't quite put a name to, but which would come to mind later producing an amusing moment.

The coach initially took us through the streets of the city, with the guide providing a commentary pointing out the places of interest. We stopped at the beautiful Black Horse Square, and had a walk around to see greater details of the statues, and buildings, plus the narrow streets nearby.

Now, it was hot, and we were on the lookout for a chance to get an ice cream but the pace of the walk, though relaxed, did not allow any time to stop and make a purchase. Eventually Debs gave up and fought with a

48

street seller to buy a refreshing cool cornet. This took some time with the obvious queue, and the group in the meantime had overtaken us. They were moving onwards to the end of the street and beginning to turn a corner. At this point I noticed the tour minder skulking some distance away, keeping a more than natural eye on Debs. I had moved ahead of her in an attempt to see where the group was going without losing sight of Debs in the ice-cream queue, and I must admit that this character was beginning to worry me. It was at that moment that I realised who he reminded me of:

The Child Catcher in the film Chitty Chitty Bang Bang!

In this situation he looked almost sinister as he tried to keep an eye on Debs, whilst also attempting to see where the tour group was going, and to remain an invisible minder. If he had worn a long coat and a hat I would probably have collapsed on the street in a fit of laughter, but I maintained some control until Debs eventually bought the ice creams and caught up with me. I giggled an explanation of what was happening whilst ensuring the Child Catcher did not hear. Both of us were now laughing as we caught up with the group, followed closely by our minder. The incident made us the guard dog's target as a possible problem, but he need not have worried, as suitably refreshed we became model tourists and stayed with our fellow passengers for the remainder of the tour.

The short walk ended at the first major point of interest, which was the Cathedral.

Now, I am not really interested in religion, and at the
time was also quite negative about architecture. My
thoughts on the purpose of churches and cathedrals
have not altered, although sometimes the buildings
themselves are now of interest. I feel uneasy about
religious buildings as I believe I am invading a place of
serious importance to many people. This is compounded
on many tours as most of them visit churches and
cathedrals believing they will appeal to tourists. In
reality I do not believe this is true with many British
tourists.

Anyway, it was culturally interesting and we were
soon back on the coach for another short trip, before
boarding a funicular railway to go further up the hill.
Here we had a quick sample of local wine and a snack,
plus a chance to look across the city, and see the
differences between the new and old parts that were a
result of a major earthquake in the past.

After the refreshment break, the coach took us back
down the hill through narrow streets lined with beautiful
buildings covered in tiles to keep the insides cool. At the
bottom of the hill we were dropped off at the shops and
had a short time to investigate and buy keepsakes.
Although the aim was to get us into the large expensive
shops, the group rebelled and quickly went its own way
to a market area where small shops sold items of much
more local interest as souvenirs.

We had decided to try and buy something small, and
local to all the places we would be visiting, and in Lisbon
this resulted in some tiled coasters embedded in local
cork. They have found a home on our living room table

and often support a glass of wine each as we re-watch videos of our holidays.

Eventually time was up and we had taken our last photographs and video clips of Lisbon. We got back on the coach for the trip back to *'Oriana'*, where the keepsakes were stored and money returned to the safe.

Lisbon was a special port, and it became one of the places with a mental tick against it for somewhere to return to. In fact the day had been very special with good weather, lots to look at, with a little amusement built in to remind us.

Now we were back on the ship that was already becoming home, and we relaxed back into a routine that was to continue for several days to come. It was time for a shower and change of clothes, and as we set sail again we said goodbye to Portugal and realised it was time to eat again.

Days at Sea

We left Lisbon floating physically on a ship, but mentally we were floating much higher in a bubble of euphoria. The dream we had had for so many months, was being surpassed in so many ways. The ship was beautiful, the food and entertainment a delight, and the people around us all made the experience so new but so natural.

A comment made by our friend Betty summed up what I had not realised. She said that when she first saw me I was tense and uncomfortable, but now I was relaxed and enjoying the holiday in the way that it was supposed to be.

A cruise ship is a floating hotel with none of the drawbacks of still being contactable by phone or letter. Normal daily troubles and interferences disappear and allow the experience to sink into and be absorbed to whatever level you want it to be.

For the next few days, we sampled the delights of what are known as 'sea days', when there are no ports to stop at, and so no disruption to the peace and relaxation of enjoying what a cruise ship has to offer.

During the night we had completed the journey down past the coast of Portugal and Spain and the next morning we turned left into the Mediterranean Sea. On the port side we caught sight of Gibraltar, while on the starboard side was North Africa. This was a rare moment when two continents can be viewed at the same time, but we were not stopping at either yet, as our next destination was the Greek Island of Santorini which required several days of sailing to reach.

I will digress again now to give a quick look at sea days, which many people perceive as a boring time, but in reality are a delight.

In our case each sea day started with an early-morning tap on the door from our cabin steward bearing a pot of tea and packets of biscuits. This enabled a slow release from sleep before deciding what to wear for the day. Sea-day clothing was normally an easy choice of which pair of shorts and which tee-shirt to select. Next came a quick check of the day's programme for anything that sparked an interest, before going for breakfast.

As we left the cabin we would hang a little sign on the door telling our steward that he could make the beds. The sign was rarely necessary as he constantly listened for doors closing to see who had left, so enabling him to pounce on a vacant cabin. During breakfast he cleaned the room and made the bed with its daytime covers to allow us weary cruisers to take a snooze without disturbing the bed too much.

We almost always took breakfast in the *Conservatory* where there is a take-away buffet that can be eaten inside or taken out onto the adjacent deck area. Alternatively we could have eaten in the restaurant with full waiter service if that had tickled our fancy. For the truly pampered cruisers, breakfast can also be delivered to the cabin, but this has a reduced choice, and also shortens our valuable vertical time for making the most of the holiday.

After breakfast the weather dictated the early morning activity. If the sun was saying hello to the world I would select a suitable pair of loungers by the pool, while Debs went back to the cabin to have a post breakfast wash and to collect sun-worship wear, towel, swimming costume, a book, plus an adequate layer of cream to negate the burning. When she returned I would go and get my bits as well, and we then relaxed for an hour or two.

Debs often had a swim for exercise, and I sometimes joined her to quickly exhaust myself, plus clearing my conscience for the excess food I had eaten. My favourite activity for that time of the morning was to rest my eyes or just watch the rest of the ship wake up. The decks were relatively quiet until mid-morning while the passengers walked first one way to breakfast and then back to grab the sun loungers. Although there were sufficient loungers for every ardent sun worshipper on board, they did become rarer as the morning progressed, and prime spots on any cruise ship are limited.

By about 11 o'clock we had often had sufficient sun, and as the decks were normally very congested by that time we would pack up and move indoors. There was almost always a port lecture during the early stages of the cruise to enlighten us on the delights of the stops coming up. If this was not the case, or the talk was about a port of no interest to us, we settled for a cup of coffee and then strolled around the shop areas, where we laughed quite openly about the excessive prices being charged. We rarely bought anything on the ship, preferring local purchases at the ports visited.

54

As lunch approached we'd go back to the cabin and pick up the daily international news-sheet for a chance to scan the headlines and more especially for me to catch up on sporting action at home.

How about the wet days?

Well to be honest our cruise was dry, hot and sunny throughout, so this was not necessary but ships cater for bad weather as well as sunny days.

On the odd day when the weather was not so pleasant things started at about 9 o'clock in the morning when a programme of activities commenced to entertain bored cruisers. Talks from guest speakers were always a good opportunity for me to have a sleep, but many people found them interesting. As an alternative there were classes where one could learn or develop dancing skills, or perhaps take part in a game of bridge. Around the ship there were unlimited places to sit and read a book, and even a small cyber cafe to surf the web or to send emails. Personally, I was using this holiday as a chance to switch off from technology, but many others found the extended isolation difficult to handle, and made full use of this facility.

As the morning progressed the activities became designed for larger gatherings with a quiz perhaps, and there was always the slot machine arcade (sorry, the casino) if that appealed. The bars were always serving coffees to meet varying tastes, but they started tempting drinkers to top up the alcohol quite early in the day.

Lunch quietly crept up on unsuspecting stomachs and as with all the meals there was a choice. There was

55

waiter service in the restaurant, or passengers could go and help themselves in the *Conservatory.* Another alternative was to grab a quick snack from the informal food venues. These were close to the pools and allowed sunbathers to avoid a break in exposure for no longer than necessary.

The 24-hour cafe offered a changing menu to suit differing tastes throughout the day. There was always a salad bar for a starter and this could be followed by a light meal, filled baguettes or maybe just soup and a roll. After that a simple dessert was available to round it all off. Of course this was all free, with the only expense being the glass of wine, or beer, soft drinks or individually prepared coffees.

This bistro-style café was one of the options that we sometimes made use of for lunch but many people went there for virtually all their meals, as the formal restaurant dining did not suit their needs.

Bing Bong...

"This is the officer of the watch"

At 12 o'clock noon, the ship's bell heralded the daily announcements of where we were and where we were going, plus an invitation to have the formal lunch in one of the restaurants.

Here traditional waiter service in air conditioned coolness treated people to a relaxed three course meal, although sometimes this was altered to a themed lunch based maybe on the Traditional English Pub meal or a seafood special. This was not favoured by ourselves except on very rare occasions, but many passengers seem to believe that all food they consumed should be selected from a menu, and brought to them by a waiter.

On several sun-filled days the pool deck hosted a barbeque or themed buffet, to enable bronzed cruisers a chance to run and grab their food whilst going into the shade for the minimum of time.

No matter where we ate, the cocktail waiters and waitresses patrolled the decks and restaurant areas continually tempting the passengers with drinks, and few could resist for the complete cruise.

Oh! I nearly forgot one eating choice.

Room Service was always available for the unsociable passengers who believed the best part of the ship was their cabin. Some people really did spend most of the day in their cabin, and for whatever reason avoided other passengers as far as possible.

...we never used Room Service!

So where did we go?

Well just like breakfast we frequented the *Conservatory* on most days. There were always a huge number of people there for lunch and although busy it was rarely uncomfortable.

Here there were two counters that were each laid out with identical choices of starters, main courses and desserts. There were hot and cold options with no limit except gravity to restrict how much could be put on a plate. The range of salad items was mouth-watering and we were normally totally satisfied with this option for our lunch.

So thirty minutes later for us, or an hour later for formal diners, the lunch was over and we started to think about the afternoon.

If the sun was tempting we found a spot close to the pool again, but this became difficult with so many other passengers having similar ideas. We occasionally found an alternative less-popular spot in the sun to sleep off the exertion of eating, or even a place in the shade when temperatures rose too far.

The saying is that the pace of the ship reduces after lunch and this was definitely true, but our metabolism is such that the need for some exercise was eventually necessary.

Sometimes the gym appealed for some serious exercise, and it was really well equipped with machines of bodily torture. Post-lunch was often a quiet time in the gym except for some of the theatre troupe stretching out out aching muscles before the next performance, plus adrenalin junkies who could not survive for long without pushing their bodies to the limit.

For the slightly less enthusiastic there were organised games in the sports nets with cricket or football, and on deck the traditional deck quoits or shuffleboard, which is a bit like a giant game of shove halfpenny with wooden blocks.

Moving down the exertion scale again you could just stroll around the decks, watch a film, go to another talk, or join in with the bridge and dancing classes again. The shops were always open with special offers to loosen the passengers' grip on their money. Alternatively there were art auctions to tempt people to spend some bigger money, and bingo where a few got some money back. As a treat we could have had our hair cut and styled, or had a massage based on the ancient arts of balancing hot stones on your back, or covering the skin in seaweed that had been marinated for several hours in a bucket of mud.

Mid-afternoon there was a chance to indulge in some more refreshments with tea and cakes.

...well you just have to sometimes don't you?

If anybody believes that they would be bored on a cruise, they should think again as it is more the case of how to fit everything in, or what to miss out.

Before we were aware of it, the evening approached and another of our daily rituals beckoned. Debs and I are quiz buffs and each day at around 5 o'clock there was an informal individual quiz to test the brain for a small prize. In simple terms it was a way of combining a pint of beer or a cocktail with a little bit of thinking thrown in. On *'Oriana'* the quiz happened in the *Lord's Tavern* where the decor and atmosphere was close to a typical pub.

The *Lord's Tavern* has a number of cricket history items such as pictures of teams and autographed bats to tempt enthusiasts of the game to look at the names and dates. On the wall is a mural of the Lords Cricket Ground with three spectators watching from the pavilion. On our cruise we heard a comment from someone that there was a man on the ship who strutted around as if he owned it. Well in fact he DID own it - he was Lord

59

Stirling, who was the chairman of P&O at the time, and he is one of those spectators depicted in the mural.

After the quiz, which Debs won on a few occasions, we went back to the cabin to have a shower and select our evening clothes. Once ready we usually had a stroll around the shops, and occasionally Debs would avail herself of the perfume samplers. This period before the first dinner sitting is a strange time on the ship, as half of the guests are in tidy, if not formal clothing, while the other half on the later dinner sitting are often still in their shorts and tee shirts.

Bing, Bong...

"The Oriental and Peninsular restaurants are now open for the first sitting of dinner."

If there is any reluctance to eat anything else for the day, then it quickly disappears as the evening meal beckons. By the third day the waiters knew us well and greeted us like old friends. We caught up with our table-mates and shared our experiences of the day, and our plans for the evening, over a multi-course meal that rarely disappointed us.

Dinner complete, it was a quick return to the cabin to turn off the lights and open the curtains so meticulously prepared by our steward, and then away to the evening entertainment. The shows and cabarets allowed us an hour to relax and begin digestion, while marvelling over the standard of entertainment provided. During this period, the second sitting of dinner was going on.

Mid-evening allowed a time to have a quiet chat with Bill and Betty, or to relax on our own in some bar, or on the aft terrace of the ship, before going to an alternative show, or for a quiet drink until the syndicate quiz rounded off the night.

Sometimes we had a quick supper of tea and sandwiches, but this was more habit than need before going back to the cabin for a quick read and a peaceful night's sleep to savour the day and dream of tomorrow.

Santorini - Wednesday 23rd August

By now the weather was glorious from early morning to nightfall and we relaxed into our holiday as we crossed the Mediterranean. Once past the Gibraltar Straits land became a rare sight except for the distant coast of Africa to the south, or occasional glimpses of faraway islands.

The only disturbances to our routine of daily sunshine intake were the gentle, almost calming, throb of the ship's engines, the regular *Bing Bong* announcements to warn us that we might be missing a meal, or a dolphin alert to direct excited cruisers to stare over one side of the ship or the other.

Having passed through the Straits of Messina with its version of a maritime traffic jam we continued into the Aegean Sea. We had already remarked on the beautiful colour of the sea in the Mediterranean but that changed now to an even more delightful blue-green mirror of water. Any thoughts we had of the cruise being a mistake were long forgotten. Books were being consumed at an alarming rate and the nooks and crannies of the ship had virtually all been explored and savoured. We had been to the different port talks and were ready for our next stop at the Greek Island of Santorini.

We were scheduled to arrive in Santorini after lunch for a half day afternoon visit, and hundreds of people assembled on the decks as the first signs of the volcanic outcrop appeared, in anticipation of what the island would offer. Small ships and ferries became more common as we got closer, and eventually the island grew from a lump on the horizon to discernible cliffs with winding roads carrying cars and coaches.

Finally *'Oriana'* stopped and dropped its anchor in the bay, and occasional sounds carried from the shore to welcome us to Santorini.

We had decided not to have an organised tour but just to go and stretch our legs and explore the town of Fira perched on the cliff above the bay where we were anchored.

This was the first chance we had to savour the thrill of using small boats to ferry us to the shore. Normally this involves the use of the on-board tender boats but here they insisted on the island's own craft. It was a surprise to be on such a small boat after the vast ship, with a lot more movement and excitement from being almost at sea level. The spray gently splashing us tickled our senses. We breathed in the familiar sea smells, and the salt left a mild taste in the mouth. It was another experience that added to the already filling catalogue of new and memorable moments that make up a cruise.

Santorini is a typical Greek tourist trap. We saw little evidence of traditional work going on in the area that we visited, but more of a well-drilled exercise in tempting holidaymakers to spend their money. When on land we had a choice of a cable car to the centre of Fira at the top of the cliffs, or to take the winding pathway either by donkey or on foot. My fear of heights dictated the pathway, and we fortunately decided to walk, as the state and smell of the donkeys were not appealing. That walk, or more accurately climb, was a lesson we learnt for later.

Firstly it was hot, in fact very hot, and although warned about covering our still-tender skin, and having lots of drinks, we were not fully prepared. The pathway zigzagged up the cliff for approaching a mile and before long we were craving shade and fluid. The situation was made worse by the regular stampede of donkeys going back down to the bottom with tourists scattering in all directions to find a safe haven. We quickly learnt to listen for the distant rumble of hooves on the cobbles giving us a few seconds warning to leap to the side or to go into the small shops that lined the path at intervals.

At the top the first priority was a cool drink and an ice cream, and a decision was made to ignore my fears and to go back down by the cable car.

Fira is beautiful with its small typically whitewashed cottages and blue roofs. Our cameras were busy capturing memories as we walked through the narrow streets or looked out from the high vantage points over the bay below. *'Oriana'* stood out as it towered over other smaller ships and local boats. The air was still and the heat almost burning our airways and we learnt our lesson about having plenty of drinks for future destinations.

We spent little more than an hour exploring Santorini before the air-conditioned comfort of the ship beckoned us back. Down the cliff we went in the cable car after queuing for several minutes, and then back onto the ferry to the ship.

The island was logged in our memory as somewhere to go back to if we ever had the chance again, although so far this has not happened.

Back on *'Oriana'* we changed our clothes and had a long cooling drink. As the afternoon continued we stared back at the island and stored our souvenirs away safely. All too soon the peace and tranquillity on board was broken by the sounds of anchors rising and announcements of our impending departure. We sailed away leaving Santorini behind us and relaxed again into the routine of eating and entertainment as we moved towards Asia and the port of Kusadesi.

Were we bored yet?

Not on your life, this holiday was as close to a dream as we could imagine.

Evenings on board

After our short stay in Santorini, *'Oriana'* set sail for Kusadesi in the Asian part of Turkey.

We were now into a series of ports each day with the ship doing its job during the nights to get between each one.

So what happens at night to make a cruise so enjoyable?

Now, Debs and I are creatures of habit, and although what I describe now was not always the case, it is typical of what we did throughout the cruise.

Late in the afternoon we went back to the cabin for a quiet moment to read a book, or in my case have a quick snooze. We both freshened up and had a shower before making our way to the Lord's Tavern for the afternoon individual quiz. This is not like the syndicate quiz, as it is far more enjoyable with twenty questions on general knowledge of a standard such that most people can answer most of the questions, with the occasional 'stumper' to sort out a winner. Debs and I always sat together and our challenge was to see who did best between us rather than winning. Sometimes Debs would succeed in winning a small prize such as a pen or umbrella but usually we were more interested in a quick drink to relax before dinner.

The timing of this quiz often caused us some stress as it finished about half an hour before our dining time. That was adequate when the dress code for the evening was casual but preparing for a formal evening, meant a much tighter timescale. Having said that, we were never late, and I believe we always looked the part and maintained the standards required.

Bing Bong...

"The first sitting for dinner is now being served in the Oriental and Peninsular restaurants."

We made our way into the *Oriental* restaurant and went straight to our now familiar table. The waiter shuffled the chair to allow Debs to sit down followed by a well-practiced flick of the napkins before laying them across our laps. The second waiter handed out the evening's menu, followed swiftly by filling our glasses with iced water and offering a bread roll while we scanned the menu for the treats on offer.

Within a couple of minutes our table friends arrived and had the same service. While decisions were being made we discussed and laughed our way through the experiences of the day. After a well-rehearsed period of time the waiter returned to take our orders, and by now we knew not to delay this to ensure we were served as quickly as possible.

Typically the starters would include an appetizer of salmon, fruit or mousse with the option of a soup course to keep our digestive system happy before the main act.

This would be a choice of different meat, fish, or vegetarian dish plus a daily speciality often based on the port of call that day. These menus were never repeated throughout the cruise but there was always the option of a standard daily list of steak, chicken or fish when nothing else appealed. The vegetables were quickly brought to the table, with a potato variant and usually three other vegetables. There was no limit even for the hungriest (or greediest) diner, but we seemed to take less each night as the cruise progressed.

By now we would have perhaps chosen a glass of wine to sip with our meal, between refreshing our palette with the never-emptying water glass. The wine was not expensive and was always of a quality to satisfy our basic knowledge of wine.

As soon as the last person at the table laid their knife and fork on the plate, our waiters returned to clear away the debris, and the menus were returned allowing us to make our choice of a dessert course. There always seemed to be sufficient space in our stomachs to select a pudding or at least ice cream. Occasionally Debs would opt for cheese and biscuits, but we could have had that as well as the puddings, with a friendly nod to the waiter.

Coffee or tea was offered to finish plus a chocolate or piece of fruit to nibble at, or to wrap in a paper napkin to take away for a midnight snack.

An hour or so after sitting down we would be struggling to our feet (assisted by the waiters), and with a friendly farewell to those around us we would quickly return to the cabin to prepare ourselves for the evening's entertainment.

This might sound so routine that it became boring, but it wasn't. I never found myself thinking that the choice was limited, and was rarely disappointed by the food on offer.

Kusadesi - Thursday 24th August

No longer in Europe, we arrived at the Asian port of Kusadesi in Turkey.

Although I had no idea of what the day would bring it was going to leave an impression that has stayed with me ever since. It brought school history to life, and expanded my mind from a disinterest in ancient ruins to a fascination of what was achieved with no more than manpower and imagination.

We woke up and breakfasted as normal but it was already apparent that this was going to be a hot day.

After booking in at the theatre for our trip, we were soon on the coach and away through the streets and onwards to the first call. This was the small town of Selcuk and the ruins of St John's Basilica. Within the site is the supposed burial site of John the Baptist. My head was spinning slightly with a confusion concerning the relevance of a burial site for a man I considered a Christian but who was also revered by Muslims.

The site itself was interesting from an archaeological perspective, with pillars of marble and remains of walls that were described by the guide in huge detail. The heat was quite dramatic and patches of shade were sought out by the guide, to allow the still rather white and delicate skins of our group to be protected, whilst at the same time allowing us to see the most interesting sites. I was busy with my video camera capturing anything that looked mildly worth remembering, and had not noticed at one point that the slab I was standing

69

on was being described as the resting place of John the Baptist. It was at that moment that I realised the magnitude of what I was seeing, and the days in school when my teachers were attempting to fill my head with history started to make a little more sense.

As well as the sites that the guide was describing I often crept away from the group to film the area around where we were standing. The poverty of the area with old buildings crammed into narrow streets, reminded me that not the entire world lives in neat detached houses. Most of the houses were built of rough stone with shuttered windows to avoid the sunlight making life unbearable. In every direction there appeared to be religious buildings and other relics consisting of just pillars or statues obviously spanning centuries of history. One pillar in particular stood alone in a field and engaged my interest. Several people were standing nearby in groups but our guide made no mention of it.

We were to come to that later.

Having completed this short visit we returned to the air-conditioned coach and slowly eased our way out of the small town and into the countryside climbing into the hills. This was a pleasant relief from the sunshine and I noticed the temperature display in the coach was registering 30°. We came to another stop with other coaches all around us where we alighted to make a short walk into a shaded glade, and another religious site known as Bulbuldagi. The trees protected us from the heat, and the mildly perfumed atmosphere from the flowers made for a relaxing walk in near silence, except for the birds singing and the gentle clicking from invisible insects around us.

The guide pointed out all manner of monuments and relics before arriving at another religious conundrum. In a very peaceful corner of the site was a small building that was declared to be the resting place of Mary, the mother of Jesus. Having explained its significance the guide allowed those who wanted the opportunity, a chance to look inside. In the middle of this Islamic country was a group of Nuns standing at the doors guarding their precious building, and silently offering head covering to the women. My mind was so confused that I didn't enter, and I waited outside as several of our group made their short pilgrimage through the house.

Nine hundred years of history had made me temporarily forget the ship, and I contemplated what I was experiencing in near silence.

As we moved on we passed a wall maybe 10 to 20 feet long, with every possible crack filled with small multi coloured pieces of material or even tissues. These represented religious offerings made by the locals to remember a friend or relation who had left this life. I felt almost ashamed that I was witnessing such faith whilst mine was so non-existent.

Still only mid-morning, and we were back on the coach (temperature now mid-30°) and off to the next stop - the ancient city of Ephasus.

It was now very hot, and sips of water (just a little tepid) were essential to avoid dehydration. Hats were firmly fixed to our heads to avoid the direct sunlight, and

: had to be regularly wiped away to avoid my
ging from the salty moisture. Debs and I had
one family whose overweight mother appeared
to be wearing a large overcoat. She never seemed to
drink anything, and her temper was worsening by the
minute as the heat sapped her strength and mind.

The site we had arrived at initially looked like a sandy
wasteland with numerous lumps of rock or bits of wall
that made little sense, but soon the guide started to
describe everything in immense detail and she brought
to life how this city looked centuries ago. It was once a
major port but an ongoing battle against silt was
eventually lost. As the water receded the city was laid to
waste, and covered in sandy deposits that gradually
buried all the buildings. Archaeologists eventually found
the site and began to uncover the remains and it left me
speechless that so much still stood after the tens of feet
of deposit had been dug away.

We started to walk down a more obvious road with
temples and forums with stone sitting areas that now
triggered the imagination. There was the remains of a
street lamp in the marble road and graffiti from
centuries ago declaring the presence of an ancient Kilroy
having been there to deface it. Elsewhere we were
directed to an ancient public toilet of stone benching
with holes to the drainage below.

As we moved further down the road a building
became visible that towered above the surrounding area
- this was the city library. When we eventually got to it,
we looked up at the amazing remnants of the building

with its ornate pillars and window spaces that had survived the passage of hundreds of years.

This was history, and it was real, and it was amazing.

Moving further down the road we rounded a corner and there was a chorus of sighs as we caught our first sight of a vast amphitheatre with rows and rows of stone benches carved into the hillside. Standing in the late morning glare and heat of the sun I gazed giddily down from near the top, and captured more video memories of a civilisation I had ignored in school, but which was now leaving a lasting impression in my mind.

A last few minutes of walking and we were at the bottom of the city and our coach was waiting to cool us down. We had forgotten that less than an hour ago a photographer had been taking pictures of the various groups of tourists as they arrived, but he now waited at the different coaches to sell us a more permanent memory of our visit to this almost indescribable piece of history.

We relaxed in the cool coach and made a short journey to a little restaurant where we were to sample some local food and wine. There was some considerable concern by many about what this would be like in comparison to the food on *'Oriana',* but in general we thoroughly enjoyed the experience, especially with a few glasses of wine to take away any worries about what we were eating. The large woman I mentioned earlier had now reached a crisis point in her dehydration and almost collapsed from the heat. She embarrassed herself, and most of our group, with a verbal tantrum until people forced her to drink and rest a while.

I remember very little of what we ate, as my mind was racing through what I had seen so far, but soon we were back on the coach waiting for the stragglers before continuing to another cultural site. The temperature finally reached 40° centigrade, and I was so glad I had replenished my bottle of water at the restaurant.

The last stop was at a partly destroyed mosque that was attached to the Museum of Ephasus. It was full of amazing statues and artefacts that had been recovered, but it could not inspire me compared to seeing remains in their original locations.

A few minutes later we took a short walk and arrived at that spot I had seen many hours ago. It was the remains of a pillar that I had filmed at our first stop, and its significance now became apparent. Only three or four metres high, the almost-destroyed pillar was the last remaining part of the Temple of Artemis, one of the Seven Wonders of the ancient world.

I stood in awe of what was just a few feet away from me. Even Debs noticed that I had gone very quiet. This was special to me, as I had read and remembered the significance of the Seven Wonders, and now to actually see one sent shivers down my very hot spine.

There was a drawing of the temple in its original glory and I could visualise this pillar being a part of it. As it was now almost completely destroyed, it increased the significance of it even more, and I've been left ever since with a vivid memory of this little piece of history.

74

After a few minutes the visit was over and we returned to the coach for a pleasant trip back to Kusadesi and *'Oriana'*.

Before the ship left the port we had a little time to explore Kusadesi, so we visited a small market near the harbour side. This was far more spectacular than I could ever have imagined, with the traders doing their best to convince us to buy their wares.

They attracted our attention, hassled us, followed us and continued to hassle, but generally to no avail. We wanted to look around, and had no intention of buying leather jackets, or *"genuine fake Rolex watches"* as one of the traders used as his sales patter. Sticking to our plans, we only bought small items and succumbed to a couple of alabaster dishes and some fresh saffron costing no more than a couple of American dollars.

Back to the ship, and it was time for our evening showers and to freshen up before dinner. We said goodbye to Kusadesi and relaxed back into the familiar luxury of the ship, as we sailed north towards Istanbul.

Istanbul - Friday 25th August

During the night we sailed north and made our way through the Dardanelles and into the Black Sea.

I had little or no knowledge of the significance of the Dardanelles, and did not pay much attention to the number of information messages being relayed to passengers about the times when we would be passing various landmarks. However, during odd moments on deck that night we could see the shore close to the ship, and the lights of monuments marking spots where battles had taken place or ships sunk.

A lot of people on that cruise were taking the opportunity to use it to visit the site where members of their family had fought, or who had died in this area either during the battle action or on ships that were lost. It was a pity that the passage was at night so not allowing a view in daylight, but the spectacle was still very moving with the memorials lit up.

In the morning we sailed on to complete the journey to Istanbul and just before lunch we moored up with all the usual activities that accompany a large ship coming to a port. This was the busiest port we were to visit on our cruise, with Asia on one side and Europe on the other. Between the two continents the Bosphorus buzzed with boats and ferries of all sizes and many of them played music as if to welcome us, although really much of it was to call the Muslim people to Friday prayers.

We moored on the European side of the city, and from our cabin we could see mosques with their domes and minarets all around us. Some were larger and could be identified on the map of the port we had been supplied with, while others were simply religious buildings for the local people. This was very different to the other cities we had visited, as typical Christian buildings no longer dominated the skyline and the air had a perceptible aroma of spices.

Istanbul was the major port of call for the cruise and we were to stay there overnight. We had two tours booked for here with one that first afternoon, and another for the next morning.

Lunch completed, we gathered all the necessary bits to cover ourselves from the sun and to avoid dehydration from the heat. Then we were off to the theatre to await the call to our first tour, which was a short coach trip and a long walk around some of the highlights of the city.

The coach took us from the dockside into the City, and even that short ride highlighted just how busy Istanbul is. Everywhere we looked there were people with barrows transporting mountains of cardboard boxes to the shops and market stalls, with even more people carrying goods away in smaller boxes or bags. Almost everyone seemed to be involved with buying or selling something.

The traffic was horrendous, but we soon came to a coach park where rows and rows of coaches were offloading or gathering hundreds of tourists. Our first visit was to Verebatan Sarayi, which is a Byzantine underground cistern. This was once the reservoir for the City, and as we descended down a series of staircases there was a noticeable difference from the outside brightness and heat into the cool gloom of the chamber.

Initially the darkness stopped us realising what was there, but as our eyes adjusted to the very low level artificial light we could make out something close to a small lake, with pillars holding up the roof that formed the floor of the building above. Our guide described what was before us, and highlighted the fact that there were 336 pillars that were all different to each other. Some had particular tales associated with them, like one that was a verdigris colour and was the only pillar with any patterning. It had peacock like swirls in the stone surface, and at one point was a well-worn area with a finger size hole into which you could stick one of your fingers and make a wish.

Umm... not sure about that, but Debs did her bit for tradition and tried it out.

For some time the semi-darkness reduced our ability to notice much, but after a while we spotted movement in the water and realised that it was full of fish. The obvious question was soon posed to our guide about the cleanliness of the water for drinking with fish swimming around in it. His reply was really quite sensible;

"If the fish are alive then the water can't be doing us much harm".

Of course in reality this lake was no longer used for the water supply, but the answer may have been true for the past when drinking water did come from here.

After about half an hour we departed the chamber and returned to the now more noticeable extreme heat of the day, and although we quickly longed to get back to the air-conditioned coach, we were in fact about to walk for a few minutes to the next attraction, which was a carpet shop. I suppose it is one of the things you just have to do when in Turkey but I am not sure if we would have put it high up on our list.

It was not really a shop but more of a theatre where we would perhaps be tempted to part with our money. Some of our tour group were offered small chairs, but many of us tried to be a little authentic and sat on cushions to watch the show. The shop owner (well that was what we were told) stood in the centre of the room while his workers brought in roll after roll of different carpets that were artistically flung onto the floor to show the variations of weave, patterns and colours that were available. It seems that different areas of the country have their own particular weave or pattern, and depending on the material used they varied in price from expensive to *"you must be kidding!"*

While this was going on, we were offered small glasses of apple tea (a Turkish delicacy) that provided a little refreshment. It was not to everyone's taste, but while I accepted it as being reasonable, Debs fell in love with it, and I had a suspicion we would be bringing some of that home with us.

The 'performance' continued and there was some interest being shown by some of the group, with questions being asked about how it could be carried away or shipped back to the UK. This resulted in another demonstration of how to take a generous sized carpet and neatly fold it over and over until it fitted in a little case that could easily have been carried away.

Smiles and applause all round.

Eventually the salesman asked if anyone was interested, or if we just wanted to look around, and this was our cue to give a final round of applause and after a token look at other carpets, we slipped out into the sunshine to await our guide. In reality we had a look around the other shops nearby and found far more interesting things, but just watching the people was an experience in itself.

At the agreed time our guide, having finished his drink and received any sales commission from the carpet shop owner, appeared at the same time as the coach pulled up and gathered up the group from various pockets of shade to make the short trip back to *'Oriana'*. We had not done very much that afternoon, but most of us were chattering and laughing about what we had seen.

Back on board the ship there was a chance to cast off somewhat *"whiffy"* clothes and to have a cool drink and a comfortable rest. The evening was to present a new experience for us, as *'Oriana'* was to remain moored up, allowing the opportunity to venture out again if we wanted to. There were no major shows or cabaret acts that night so it was also the chance for some of the crew to stretch their legs on shore, and I can imagine that this is quite a treat for the 24/7 types of people who work on cruise ships. However, not all of the entertainment staff could have this perk, as the ship was to have a special late night party on the deck in the moonlight, that we had been told would be spectacular.

We were soon ready for our evening meal having suitably showered, quizzed, and cocktailed.

Evening in Istanbul

Highlights of the menu for that evening.

Diced Avocado with Crabmeat and Marie Rose Sauce
Penne Pasta Sakura
Galantine of Duck with Orange Salad and Warm Toast

∞

Parsnip and Apple Soup
Consommé of Chicken Celestine

∞

Poached Supreme of Salmon
Roast Loin of Pork
Tagiatteli Pasta Carbonara
Braised Breast of Goose with Pan Juices and Sausage Meat Stuffing
Sauté of Mushroom Stroganoff

∞

Batons of Carrots   Courgettes Rissolée and Boiled Potatoes

∞

Bread and Butter Pudding with Cream
Mississippi Mud Pie with Créme Anglais
Apricot Pavlova with Pineapple Coulis
Vanilla, Strawberry, and Rum & Raisin Ice Creams
Fresh Fruit Salad
Lemon Sorbet

∞

A selection of Cheeses and Biscuits
Fresh Fruit or Coconut Candy
Coffee or Tea

This was not one of the special or themed menus that appeared on the handful of formal nights, but I would imagine most people would find something to their liking from the offerings above.

For those people who had particular dietary requirements the ship had a team of specialist chefs who prepared such meals, with personal menus offered each evening ready for the next day. These menus had choices just like ours, but the crew did need some notice to prepare such individual dishes.

After dinner we went back to the cabin to perform our routine of opening the curtains, moving the chocolates from the pillows (in case we forget them later) and switching off the excess lights that our steward had so carefully left for us. A few minutes later we were strolling around the ship as dusk quickly turned into darkness. All around us the city had spotlights illuminating major landmarks, especially the mosques. It was quite eerie seeing the silhouettes of crane-birds against the brightly lit buildings as they flew around the city. On board the ship we could see the preparations for the party, with coloured spotlights brightening up the main pool area, and unexplained strings crossing the decks. Although some background music was being played, the party was not due to start until much later, so we moved on and decided to take a walk on the harbour side.

The usual security was in place on the gangplank, where we had to show our cruise cards when leaving and returning, but it was generally much more relaxed with just a few people coming and going rather than major tour groups. On the harbour there were a couple of duty free shops open and attracting a few customers, but there was little to interest us especially as we would be visiting the famous Grand Bazaar tomorrow.

The major attraction for us and a few other passengers was just wandering up and down and staring up at 'Oriana'. This was the first and only time we saw her from the shore while it was lit up. 'Oriana' is a truly beautiful ship (perhaps I am biased!) and seeing her now with her flood-lighting emphasising her lines, and coloured lights reflecting in the water, it was impossible to prevent a sigh of delight. Anyone on shore near the port could not fail to be impressed, and the sight must have been equally spectacular for the hundreds of boats moving up and down the adjacent waterways.

We spent perhaps half an hour looking at the ship from different angles and taking photographs and video memories. One very memorable view was that of the restaurant at the stern of the ship where we ate each evening, and which was now full of the second sitting diners, enjoying the same menu that we had worked our way through a couple of hours earlier.

By now it was gone 9 o'clock and getting cool so we decided to return on board and have a glass of wine. We had not been excited by the idea of the party earlier, so we went into Andersons for a quiet drink and chat about Istanbul. It is a city that cannot fail to leave an impression on people, and although that impression may not be so favourable to everyone, we were amazed and looking forward to another taste tomorrow.

The bar was quiet that evening, and we soon realised that the party was probably under way, so we decided to give it a go. Returning first to the cabin to grab a jumper (most unusual on that cruise) we returned to the pool area.

Now we understood the quietness of the rest of the ship as it looked like almost everyone was crowded around the pool area. On deck, tables and chairs had been laid out and they were all occupied. On the upper areas more chairs had been laid out and these were also taken, with other people standing to watch the fun below.

We squeezed into a corner on the deck in time to sample the action, with the ship's band running through its party repertoire to back up the cruise director, the other entertainment staff and the theatre group, who were drumming up a very good atmosphere. Various loud and mildly drunken renditions of "We Are Sailing" or "Land of Hope and Glory" announced to Istanbul that the British were in port. Then came the finale of the evening. A Caribbean-style song was getting almost everyone joining in with the words, and many stood and danced along with the beat. We now discovered the reason for the strings across the deck.

Streamers had been given to everyone, and we were now told to throw them upwards on a count of three. At the appointed moment probably a thousand streamers spiralled up into the darkness. They returned into the light and many were caught by the strings. This created a brightly coloured web that entangled the people as they waved their arms, sang, laughed, and danced with excitement.

We had not brought our cameras and so have no record of that moment, but it was certainly unforgettable.

As the evening wound down we had a late night cup of tea with a couple of sandwiches (well, you have to, don't you?) before settling down in the cabin for the first night since the dream started without the now-familiar movement of the ship.

Second Day in Istanbul

The lack of movement through the night had been unusual, but the familiarity of our temporary bed allowed us a good night's sleep. This was the case for virtually the entire cruise, as the freshness of the days at sea and the busy days in port, all led us to be quite exhausted by the time we relaxed our heads onto our pillows.

It was Saturday the 26th August and as we woke and climbed the staircases to breakfast, there was a more than usual spring in our steps with the expectations of another day in Istanbul. The tours were starting early that day and far more people were up and eating in the *Conservatory* buffet than we had seen before. We were expected in the Theatre Royal by 7:45 to get our tickets for a morning tour looking at some of the major buildings of the city.

Sun cream applied, and suitably kitted out with hats, cameras, and water bottles, we were very soon climbing onto a coach for the journey to the first landmark. Istanbul was already wide-awake and once again there was the two-way traffic of barrows and people with goods to sell and others carrying their purchases home.

Out of the coach and away from its air-conditioning we felt the early morning heat of a Turkish sun, but that was soon forgotten as we walked along the road for a short distance to the area known as the Hippodrome, and the sight of an Egyptian obelisk said to be some 3500 years old. This rectangular stone pillar was a simple object, maybe 60 feet high, with a pointed top and inscriptions on the faces probably welcoming the people of Egypt to some well-known temple or theatre, or maybe the directions to some ancient fast-food bar. Those people could never have imagined that their pillar would one day be taken away and transported hundreds of miles to Istanbul (or whatever it was called then) to become a daily attraction to thousands of tourists. Its age and simplicity made it special, but so many of the treasures and buildings we saw in Istanbul were also oh-so-special.

At the other end of the Hippodrome area was another pillar, but this time it was of a hollow tube construction and was the colour of verdigris and adorned with patterns. It had been damaged in the past and now had a gaping hole, but this made it no less attractive, especially as it was again thousands of years old. The pillar had its base in a circular pit about ten feet deep that was surrounded by a waist-high metal railing fence. This was presumably to protect it from any further damage, but as we gathered close to look at its detail we could see a vagrant sleeping peacefully in the pit, oblivious to the chatter of guides from all over the world, and the attention of cameras capturing his image. Perhaps he was just tired, but I suspect his ability to remain undisturbed was probably due to the influence of something less innocent.

From the Hippodrome our group made its way along a pathway the width of a road along with hundreds of other tourists. Each tour group had a guide carrying a little sign or coloured parasol as a magnet to attract straggling guests. There were people from a multitude of different nationalities demonstrating the universal appeal of the city. Our guide was kitted out with a small white sign showing the P&O flag and the number of our particular tour. It was not A1 for us today as that tour was yesterday, and its actual number has long been forgotten.

We were on our way to the Hagia Sophia, which is a major museum that started out as a church and then became a mosque. Its features had changed over hundreds of years to match its religious standing, and now it has multiple domed roof sections and is surrounded by four minarets.

Once inside, its vastness absorbed the hundreds of tourists without appearing crowded. It was breathtaking, with religious paintings and artefacts in every available nook and cranny, including absolutely huge urns probably over ten feet tall, covered with brightly painted decorations. In the centre of the building we looked up to the domed ceiling painted with more religious scenes, picked out with gold leaf that shone in the rays of the sunshine which came in through vast stained glass windows.

The only minor distraction was that due to damage some years ago the building was being repaired and restored to its former glory, but this involved the use of a scaffolding tower that obscured probably a third of this central area. I am sure this work will have taken a long time to complete, but I don't expect it has taken away the splendour of the Hagia Sophia for the tens of thousands of tourists who visit it each year.

Back out into the heat we followed our guide, with whom many people were now having a chat about the city and his life. He had recently left the army (all men in Turkey are conscripted for a period of time) and in near-perfect English he discussed the quite major topic of the disputes with Greece over the sovereignty of Cyprus, as well as telling us more mundane facts and stories about his home.

Our next stop was the Mosque of Sultan Ahmed, more commonly known as the Blue Mosque.

This is the largest mosque in Istanbul and consists of a huge domed area for worship in the middle, surrounded by smaller domed areas that radiate out in a number of circles that reduce in size towards the outside. Six minarets to signify its importance then surround it.

Before we entered, our guide pointed out the toilets just in case anyone needed them. A minor stampede moved towards the small buildings and at the door to the "Gents" we saw an extremely old woman collecting the entrance fees. It was only the equivalent of a few pence but some of us were caught unaware. One person was rather desperate and shoved a note (worth less than 50 pence) into the old lady's hand and walked in to do his business. The attendant shouted and waved in annoyance at this action and muttered as she continued to collect our fees.

Inside we stood to attention and relieved ourselves at remarkably clean urinals in the immaculately cared for toilet. I was standing next to the gentleman who had been in so much of a hurry, and out of the corner of my eye I saw the old lady appear, tap him on the shoulder and silently give him his change before walking away again. She was not embarrassed, but he was, and the rest of us who witnessed the incident roared with laughter.

After that little adventure we returned to our group, removed our shoes, and went inside the Mosque. The central area is enormous and the walls are covered in blue patterned tiles that reflect the light from the stained glass windows, hence the name Blue Mosque.

It is magnificent and very beautiful, with the worship area covered in prayer mats. All around, the structure has a generous number of windows that give sufficient bright and colourful light, and this is increased by strings of small lanterns over the prayer mats. Unfortunately, the sight of a man cleaning the carpet with an ageing electric vacuum cleaner rather destroyed some of the magic.

Each of the other domed areas are smaller prayer or worship areas with artefacts to display the importance to all who enter... and hundreds of tourists were entering!

There was no time to stay long as we had to be on our way again to walk to another major attraction. We strolled along the pathways and our guide was in demand once again to answer inquisitive cruisers' questions about Istanbul, and a growing number of concerns about the Grand Bazaar that most of us would be visiting later.

After walking for about ten minutes we passed through an arched entry into a much more peaceful place, with pathways shielded from the sun by trees. It felt completely different and peoples' voices become quieter to match the surroundings. We all subconsciously began to relax relaxe as we approached the Palace of Topkapi.

This is now a museum, but it was the home of the Sultans for hundreds of years and it displays the wealth they had accumulated, and the treasures they had acquired. The buildings themselves are magnificent enough, but we gasped at the sights as we moved from room to room. There was the furniture, made from precious metals and embedded with jewels, then clothing with gold stitching (plus jewels of course), or how about the actual jewellery with examples of every stone that I had heard of, but oh so much bigger than I had ever seen, with rubies, emeralds and diamonds the size of golf balls.

Outside, the buildings were themed on different cultures that had interested the Sultans enough to have them recreated at home. There were fountains (gold obviously) to cool the air in a tiled shelter surrounded by gardens that were kept green and lush like an oasis compared to the rest of the city we had seen so far.

Left to our own devices for the last few minutes we found a high vantage point overlooking the waterways of Istanbul across the Bosphorous to Asia beyond. The view was hazy now from the heat, and this late morning heat was energy sapping.

In about two hours we had visited three major buildings all within easy walking distance of each other, and although our stays were short it enabled several hundred British tourists a chance to get a flavour of the history of Istanbul and Turkey. We were now off on the final leg of our tour back through the city to the famous Grand Bazaar, which is not just somewhere to buy things but is a tourist attraction in its own right.

Through the crowded streets we walked, fending off regular attempts by the traders to tempt us to stop and look at their wares. We avoided their entreaties as suggested by our guide as time prevented any delays to the schedule.

Someone said you could buy anything in Istanbul. As we arrived at the Bazaar I realised the possible truth behind that statement. This was not just a market; it was a small town of tiny shops packed with almost anything you could imagine. Having been given a brief introduction to the bazaar we were left to our own devices for thirty minutes to wander and just be entertained by the atmosphere, or to buy some things to remind us of the experience.

Some of the shops were quite professionally designed, but these were generally the major ones selling leather jackets or high-value watches and jewellery. Others could not be described as either 'designed', or tidy, and consisted in the main as mere shelters where objects could be hung from ceilings, or stacked one on top of the other for shoppers to feast their eyes until something they wanted was seen.

We were approached by many of the traders, with some seeming quite surprised and possibly almost angry that we would not accept their invitation to view their shops.

Some were quite amusing and one actually asked me "*May I hassle you?*"

We were only there for a short time and although amused by the traders' attempts, we did not go into many shops. There were a few successes for the sellers, as we bought some small alabaster dishes, and a chess set in the same material. Debs bought some apple tea as I expected she would after yesterday's visit to the carpet shop. All in all I think we did very well avoiding the "*hard sells*".

Oh yes I also bought a fez… well why not?

The end of the tour approached and our group, some overloaded with packages, gathered at the appointed place and time before making our way back to '*Oriana*'. As we arrived at the dockside our guide thanked us for visiting Istanbul and we all applauded a very well educated and efficient guide.

Presents stored away (well, thrown on the bed actually), we hurried to the *Conservatory* for some lunch, as we were keen to go back on shore to look around a little more by ourselves. So less than an hour later we were wandering through the back streets near the docks, where we found a small number of shops offering virtually everything again, but this was more a chance to wander on our own rather than looking for things to buy.

Now, it was still very hot, but as we returned toward the dock there was a very strange experience. Virtually unnoticed, the sky had darkened and there was a cool breeze blowing. Within seconds (it seemed) it started to rain and then hailstones the size of marbles made the road white, accompanied by thunder and lightning. This was the first moment of damp weather we had had since we left Southampton, and we scampered for shelter under a shop's awning. But as quickly as it had started, the rain and hail stopped again and almost immediately the sunshine returned. Even in those five minutes the roads had become flooded, and a local taxi driver spotted a possible fare, and offered to take us to the other side of the road where the dock gate stood. This was less than 50 metres away so we declined his very kind offer and continued to shelter under the blind of a yet another "*genuine fake watch*" shop. The shop owners had realised we were not interested in making a purchase, and left us to laugh until the floods had subsided sufficiently to move on.

Finally back on board the ship we relaxed in the afternoon sunshine that was not interrupted by cloud or rain again. As the time for the ship's departure approached, more and more tour groups returned with their memories and packages from Istanbul. One group had been on a boat trip on the Bosphorous and their memory of the storm was of a moment of madness, being soaked to the skin and pelted with hailstones, with no shelter for those on the top of the boat. They were all laughing about it now. I never heard any negative comments about the city, although I wasn't actively listening for them, and I believe that these two days had been an unforgettable experience for all the first timers to the city, and probably a pleasant reminder for those returning to Istanbul.

That evening we took our departure and many people stood on deck waving as we turned around and headed down the Bosphorous and back out of the Black Sea. This was the moment where we started the return trip towards home. There may have been the first twinge of sadness, but there was still a week to go and other places to visit, so we just forgot our concerns and carried on enjoying ourselves.

The Evening Entertainment

An evening on board *'Oriana'* had more than eating and quizzes to keep us amused and occupied. The formal shows and cabaret were of course the major attraction.

On several nights the theatre was filled to overflowing with the guests watching the musical shows put on by the troupe of on-board entertainers. These were often based on existing West End shows, or themed on a particular producer, or perhaps a decade or type of music. The singers were all of a high standard and were accompanied by nimble dancers with multiple costume changes throughout the typically 45-minute shows.

I took the opportunity to visit the back-stage area one afternoon, to experience the chaos that must occur during the shows, with quite limited changing areas and rail upon rail of costumes lined up in the required order. This visit also described the very professional sound and lighting system in use, and to be honest it was better than many small theatres dotted around the UK.

As well as these shows there were a number of cabaret artists, to sing to us or play recitals for those who enjoy them, but two people stood out from the rest for our personal tastes.

The first was Gary Wilmott who is a singer, dancer, and comedian. We had already seen him many years before on one of our early Pontins holidays, when he was just starting out in the business. Since that time he had gained a much higher stature with West End shows such as 'Me and My Girl' and television work. Now, we do not normally go for singers, but knowing the name from the past, we decided to watch him.

His act had not changed significantly from when we saw him before, but the standard had certainly gone up. He was funny, even if some of the jokes were a little old, but the singing was exceptional. One of the songs was from a role he had performed and was a rendition of 'Mr Bojangles'. It was his finale and for whatever reason it hit the spot with me, and I listened with a smile as he sang and gently danced his act to an end.

Since that time whenever I hear the first few bars of that tune, I think back to his act, and of course the images of *'Oriana'* flood back.

We had a chance to speak to Gary later in the cruise and we pointed out that we had seen him at Pontins. He asked if the act had changed much, and when we said that it was similar, he smiled as if to indicate that he agreed with us.

Anyway he had another spot later in the cruise, and I was obviously not the only person to enjoy 'Mr Bojangles', as he sang it again because of the feedback he had been given.

The second person we both enjoyed was the resident comedian Nicky Martyn. Most ships at that time had a resident comedian, who stayed on board for a few weeks before swapping with another to avoid too much familiarity. Cruises are perfect for comedy as the acts normally include many jokes concerning such things as the cabins, the toilet systems, speed of the stewards to clean the cabins, waiters who whip the plates away before the fork is dropped, and of course the captains messages.....*Bing Bong.*

Debs and I were in fits of laughter as so many things that he talked about were real to us from our own experiences, and thoughts from the cruise so far. I have no doubt many of the jokes were similar to other jokes that seasoned cruisers had heard before, but it was all new to us and we had tears in our eyes and aching ribs when the act was over. He also did another spot later in the cruise, and like Gary Wilmott the audiences filled the venues to prove their popularity.

Other acts did not appeal to us but many people went to listen to the female singer and the solo musicians who performed classical sessions. Not our cup of tea, but it did show us the wide range of entertainment that a cruise offered.

We watched all the shows and cabaret acts that we could, and although the theatre held some 500 people, and the *Pacific Lounge* review bar maybe another 200 people in comfort, there were rarely more than a few seats left by the time the lights dimmed and the curtains went back.

We are often asked *"didn't you get bored on a ship?"*........ not on your life!

Mytilene - Sunday 27th August

Exactly one month since my birthday, and it felt like the holiday was one continuous bag of presents, as each day I unwrapped another one, with no disappointments.

Our stay on the Greek Island of Lesvos was at the port of Mytilene where we anchored in its bay, and used a tender boat to take us to and from the harbour. We had not booked any tour here as nothing inspired us amongst the choices, but with hindsight perhaps this was a minor mistake.

In our usual way we had breakfast and a leisurely wash and looked at the island from the ship. With all our bits and pieces ready we waited until the *Bing Bong* invitation to proceed ashore was announced. We always tried to grab an early boat to shore, to soak up the atmosphere of a new place before it got busy with too many tourists.

When we arrived ashore we had suspicions that there must have been a good party on in the town the night before, because now the place was deserted. There were a few fishermen on the quayside mending nets or preparing to go to sea, but the only other locals we saw were sitting in small café bars. Except for these cafes, the only other businesses open were an occasional tobacconist and newspaper shops.

So that day we learnt a useful fact about Greek islands. They treat Sunday in a far more religious way than is the case in the majority of British towns and cities. We had no idea if the rest of the island was buzzing with activity, but we did know that the town of Mytilene was closed.

We wandered around the harbour, which was truly beautiful and made even more so by the peacefulness, with only a few cars and scooters interrupting the sounds of the water gently lapping against the walls, or gulls crying in the hopes of titbits of fish from the small boats. After half an hour or so the town did start to show more signs of life and we sat and relaxed in the sunshine with a coffee. Looking back across the harbour to *'Oriana'* in the bay beyond, it no longer seemed quite so disappointing.

Strolling back we took a detour away from the harbour side and turned into the streets of the town, hoping to find some shops open where we could find a keepsake to buy. Initially none of the businesses were open, but eventually as we investigated the narrow twisty streets, more shops appeared and some actually had their doors open. We never went very far into the town and I am sure that if we had persisted, our retail craving would have been satisfied with larger shops, but those we did eventually find were sufficient.

The half a dozen or so shops open for customers were mainly tourist-based, but much of the stock we saw had a religious flavour, or were imported bits and pieces we could have got anywhere. The local pottery we sought was proving difficult to obtain. By now we had walked through the streets to a point almost directly behind where we had landed perhaps an hour and a half earlier, but as we turned the last corner to return to the harbour side, we saw a small shop that had a mixture of wooden and pottery items, together with typical local wine and food. The smell of olives and cheese, and the immaculately wrapped keepsakes that we bought satisfied our needs and we completed the last few steps to the tender boat embarkation point.

Soon we were purring across the bay towards *'Oriana'* for lunch and a quiet afternoon of relaxation in the sunshine, to reflect not just on Mytilene but all the places we had been to so far. It had been ten days since we left Southampton, and the experience had changed my life forever, and I believe Deb's as well.

Athens - Monday 28th August

The next morning we woke up and from the cabin window we could see the port of Pireaus, which was the landing site to get to Athens.

We had another tour booked, and after a quick breakfast it was back to the theatre to get our tickets and await our call to the coach. Athens was not very far away from the port, but the coach ride took us on a scenic drive through the local sites of Pireaus before taking us to the capital city of Greece.

Our first stop was at the Acropolis and its Parthenon, and I caught a glimpse of the Parthenon in the distance as our coach meandered through the city streets. This was yet another moment to remember, as even with my ignorance of history and geography, the Parthenon building was something I recognised instantly. The early morning sun made the stonework glow and once again the back of my neck tingled with excitement.

After a few more minutes of climbing the narrow twisting roads towards the Acropolis we arrived in the coach park. We had arrived in time to be some of the first people into the ancient site that day, so missing the major crush of tourists plus the worst of the heat to come. As we climbed the steps and entered the site the view before me instantly triggered a sense of magic. I once again marvelled at the architecture of our ancestors and wondered in awe at how all this could have been achieved without the modern cranes, transporters, and equipment that would be needed to erect such buildings today.

Our guide was another passionate person who brought the site to life with her descriptions of the Parthenon, and other temples that almost littered the area. Stories and factual information fascinated me and made me realise that the designer had planned his legacy to the world to be so unique, that no-one could ever fail to be impressed, nor to leave without a feeling of utter amazement. An example is that each pillar of the Parthenon is different in some way to the others, with no gap between them the same.

Considering the hundreds of years that had passed since its construction, the remains have stood the passage of time and I had to get quite close to the huge statues to notice their features had been weathered. Each time the guide encouraged me to turn my gaze in another direction, yet more sights made me gasp, and the camera rarely had a moment to rest.

After the formal guided tour we were given a few minutes to wander and reflect on the history before us, and we hardly spoke except to point something out that might have been missed. Our time at the Acropolis quickly ran out, and we returned to the meeting point to walk back to the coach. Looking back at the site I was sad at leaving, as I believed I would never see it again, but there was also a tingle of excitement, that unlike many millions of other people, I had at least been there.

Down from the Acropolis we arrived outside a recommended souvenir shop, where wallets and credit cards excitedly bought memories to take away. Every tour guide seems to have a particular *"recommended"* shop, and while the smiling assistants tempted us, the guides always disappeared into a back room until the tills stop ringing and then reappeared with a slightly fuller wallet. As with most of our shopping sprees, we bought some pottery (which might have been Greek) and a small bronze statuette of an ancient Olympic discus thrower. Debs and I normally bought things as a joint decision, but on this occasion I could not resist buying myself a small bust of Sophocles, which sat on my desk at work until the day I retired.

Fifteen minutes later we moved on again to fulfil another dream, with a visit to the original Olympic Stadium.

The stop at the Olympic Stadium was short but oh, so sweet.

It is an open stadium that basks in the sunshine with banked marble seating all around, and does not look in the least like a modern stadium. Its simplicity somehow personifies what the Olympics are supposed to be all about, and allows the sport to be the focus rather than the architect's vision. At the time I was not sure how much the stadium was still used for sport, but it did have a well-maintained track, so obviously it was active.

As I entered the stadium area I spotted plaques engraved with the dates and names (in Greek) of all the cities that have held the modern games. I was mesmerised by this simplicity and thought back to all the sporting moments I could remember from the Olympics

105

of my lifetime. The games have always been a highlight every four years that I look forward to, and I am always prepared to stay up late at night to watch them on the television.

While I looked at the memorabilia, Debs had walked down the sprint lanes of the track to the finish line, and I could see that she had entered into her own little dream bubble. While much younger, she had taken part in pre-Olympic trials for the 100metres, and although not quite fast enough she has retained a similar love for the games as me.

All too soon our time at the stadium was up, and I tried to attract Deb's attention, but by now she was sitting in the terraces close to the finish line, and her mind was clearly concentrating on what was before her, and not on me waving frantically at the other end of the stadium. She was finding it very difficult to come away, and I can only imagine her thoughts, but I do know that this experience was a dream come true for both of us.

Eventually we moved away from the stadium and completed the rest of our tour of Athens, by driving through the city to see its various highlights. The city impressed me with its cleanliness and the mix of modern and older buildings. The sunshine made them all the more spectacular, and like virtually all the places we had been to so far, a mental note was made of hoping maybe one day we could go back.

As we relaxed back on the ship later that afternoon we talked about the last few days, and although our words are long forgotten, I am positive that at some point we discussed how we could ever go home and not find a way of going on another cruise. As I have already said so many times, this was not just a holiday, it was a series of dreams and wishes that had been fulfilled, and we had been away for less than a fortnight of our lifetimes.

Before we knew it, the ship was slipping its moorings and gliding away from Pireaus in the late afternoon sun. I was a different person than that man who boarded *'Oriana'* a couple of weeks earlier. Although still excited as every new day brought new experiences, I had also gone through a change in my appreciation of what was happening. I liken it to being in a situation where you have a chance to have as much of your favourite food as you want. Initially you greedily gobble the food but you only taste the most obvious flavours, but eventually you relax and become able to take, your time and savour every subtle changing mouthful.

Athens was now suitably digested, and we had another quiz, another meal, and another show to prepare for as we started the westward journey across the Mediterranean to our last stop at Gibraltar in three days time.

Feeling at home

By now we felt like seasoned cruisers. We were treating the ship like a home, doing what we wanted, and what we liked from all the things that were on offer. We didn't feel obliged to do everything that was on the daily programme, and now had the confidence to ignore recommendations for particular shows or demonstrations. Our choice was often based on what we had enjoyed so far, believing that we ought to make the most of these things while we still had the opportunity.

Our eating habits did not vary much, and we never did have breakfast in the formal restaurants as we thoroughly enjoyed the "do-it-yourself" buffet style in the *Conservatory*. Our lunches were virtually all taken in that same place but I believe there were a couple of visits to the restaurant for lunch, and we also sampled the café-style option. Dinner on the other hand was taken on all but one night, in the formal surroundings with Sheila and Jim, our fellow newcomers. There was just one warm evening when Debs and I had a special dinner out on deck in the *Horizon Grill,* where we were served at a more leisurely pace by more attentive waiters as we watched the sun set and the stars appearing overhead. There was a surcharge for this meal, but it was minimal for such an intimate evening with the food cooked especially for us, and with a little more time between courses to relax and chat and giggle about our dream holiday.

Throughout the cruise the weather never let us down, and except for the short snappy shower in Istanbul, the skies were clear and the sun shone brightly and hot from the morning we arrived in Lisbon, until the morning after we left Gibraltar on the way home. I don't remember a single day when we didn't spend time in the sun to catch up on what we had missed for so many years by staying in Britain for our holidays. We were careful though, and avoided overdoing the tanning, and often found a shady place to relax rather than toasting ourselves to excess. The ship was full of experienced cruisers who spent every possible minute soaking up the sun, from the moment they rolled out from breakfast (usually late morning) until they eventually had to change for dinner. They didn't look any happier than we were, and we certainly didn't look as *"crinkly"* as some of these people looked after many years of roasting themselves.

Our cabin was near the stern of the ship and allowed us to easily get to one of the aft decks. I believe that these are the most beautiful areas of *'Oriana',* where we spent a lot of relaxing lazy moments. The view from the rear of a ship has so many adjectives associated with it that it is difficult to find a single way of describing it. If you consider some that I have heard - beautiful, dramatic, stunning, awe-inspiring, relaxing, - you might realise that it means different things to different people.

The scene is simple in its makeup, with a vast expanse of sea that changes colour according to the depth, its stillness, or the light afforded by the time of day. Now break the stillness of that scene with the wake from the ship, beginning first with lines of powerful white frothy explosions. The energy that is pushing you through the sea quickly spreads its anger into the water, becoming waves radiating away from the ship that reduce in magnitude to just lines of disturbance in the distance, before eventually becoming absorbed by the sea. This never ending evidence of power remains visible for perhaps a mile behind a ship, and I doubt any passenger with the gift of sight has not stood and watched the scene with some form of pleasurable emotion.

Even ignoring the wake, the sea has a strange effect on many people. It can change from a wallowing calm sea, to the unbelievable chaos of a storm, sending waves in all directions that lift and drop the ship like a ping-pong ball. In the middle of this energy spectrum the water can change from an almost grey colour, and then start to sparkle as the sun catches the ripples, with rainbows appearing from almost nowhere in the spray as the waves break against the ship's hull. With bright sunlight the water changes hue through various blues and greens, and of course there is the occasional bonus of a dolphin or whale who might give a solo performance, for those lucky enough to be looking in the right direction. The cost of the cruise may seem expensive, but this show is provided by nature for free.

If you can imagine this scene as a stage of a theatre, then the stern of 'Oriana' is the auditorium. It has been designed as a series of horseshoe-shaped balconies rising from the promenade deck through five levels, giving uninterrupted views of the performance of the sea. The act changes according to the time of day, or the direction of travel, or the roughness of the sea, but there is one

110

very special moment that seasoned cruisers yearn to see regularly. From this theatre, at dusk as *'Oriana'* sails eastwards on a warm Mediterranean evening, the sun sets mid-stage. It metamorphoses through a paint box of colours and shades over maybe 30 minutes as it says goodbye to you and hello to someone else. There are not many sights better than this as you lean against a rail on the stern, with a gentle cooling breeze ruffling your hair, while you sip a glass of wine. If the ship is sailing westwards then you have to put up with the moon taking its place on the stage, casting its eerie white light over the water and its audience. Not a bad alternative really, so make sure you see both if you have the chance.

Our handy access to the stern meant we could quickly check it out in the daytime for spare sun beds on our deck, and if none were available we could go up or down the levels for a spot that matched our needs. Usually this was to find a place to enjoy the sunshine, but shade was also needed sometimes as a pleasant relief from the heat on many late afternoons. If this area was too busy, as was very often the case, we could climb up the steps to the lido deck and the swimming pool areas.

This was normally our early morning point of leisure after breakfast. Reading a book or just people-watching allowed the sun's rays to first warm and then be absorbed by the skin, so a quick immersion in the swimming pool was often required now and then. At times we spent more time in the pool to swim for exercise, although in reality it was swimming from Debs, and slightly controlled floundering by me. There are three pools on *'Oriana'*. The one at the stern was

111

primarily for families but there were two in the main lido area. We favoured the *Riviera Pool* that is for adults only, and thus tended to be quieter than the *Crystal Pool*. I am not suggesting the children on board were a problem, but there comes a time in your life when a nap in the sun, really doesn't need to be disturbed by small excited screaming machines. I have been there and enjoyed the experience, so I now happily pass that stage of life to other people.

When both the stern and the other pool areas had no vacant spaces, our next option was to take a look at *Promenade Deck*.

This is a major feature of some cruise ships that gives the passengers a chance to have a stroll, hence the name. On *'Oriana'* this deck allows an unbroken circumvention of the ship, being ten feet or more wide except at the extreme stern and bow ends, where it narrows as it passes under the structure of the vessel. Its width is sufficient for passengers to relax on chairs or stretch out on recliners without disturbing the strollers, and the occasional more energetic *"power walkers"*. This last group of people find pleasure late into the afternoon by continued marching around the ship, knowing that three times around *Promenade Deck* is about one mile. Just watching them repeatedly passing by, was enough to break me into a sweat.

...best not to look too closely, just close your eyes and relax!

A benefit of a deck that goes around the ship is that often one side is in the sun, whilst the other is shaded.

Hence you have a choice of hot and cool. From my experience it is certainly easier to find a shaded spot, as most people really do overdose themselves on sunshine.

If we had still not found a suitable place, there were nooks and crannies at the bow end that were usually available, as they did suffer from a breeze that could be pleasant, but which also disturbed the sun worshippers a little. Just to upset those who might wish to re-enact the scene from the film *"Titanic"*, you cannot actually get right to the *"pointed end"* as that tends to be where a lot of the operational technical bits and pieces of the ship are sited. I also think it could put off the crew, if they had to watch endless queues of Kate Winslets and Leanardo DiCaprios risking their lives!

Failing all other options, we would sit inside in various quiet and not-so-quiet areas. Maybe we'd have a cup of coffee with some Belgian chocolates, or if it was close to lunch perhaps a pint of lager at the bar, or a glass of wine late in the afternoon. I will say that although coffee was quite a regular treat, drinking alcohol during the day was very rare for us. You really can drink a lot, as well as eating mountains, unless you set unwritten rules in your heads to control potential greed.

So having left Athens you now have an idea of how we spent the two full days, and another morning, as we came away from the Aegean Sea and back into the Mediterranean. We once more caught a distant glimpse of Africa, on our port side this time, and on the Thursday morning Europe became visible on the starboard side as we neared Gibraltar.

Debs and I had gone to the port talk to hear about Gibraltar, and to consider if we should go on any of the tours. As the visit was only for the afternoon we decided to just walk into the town, and perhaps take a look at the Duty Free shops for last-minute presents.

As Thursday morning progressed the horizon's silhouettes got bigger and eventually the shape of the famous Rock of Gibraltar became obvious.

...time for lunch.

Gibraltar - Thursday 31st August

Our early lunch was quickly over and we watched the docking routine for the last time. This quite short visit made us realised just how busy Gibraltar is as a trading port for fuel, oil and commodities, as well as for ferries on the way to and from the African ports. The sun was still shining and we had been warned that the temperature would be quite high that day so we should all be careful. Many of the passengers had decided to delay their lunch until going ashore, and having Gibraltar's famous "English Lunch". I think this was more of a custom rather than a treat as a pint of lager with a plate of fish and chips rarely springs to the top of my choices. Besides, *'Oriana'* had fish and chips on the menu that day and lager was always available.

Soon the ship was tied to the dock and permission had been given for us to go ashore. We bounced our way down the gangplank for the penultimate time.

As we walked from our maritime parking spot onto the main dock road, we saw another cruise ship berthed on the other side of the terminal building from ourselves. There was however a significant difference in the two ships. This ship was from the Thomson fleet, and although perfectly adequate to do its job, it was tiny in comparison to *'Oriana',* which was casting a shadow over the complete vessel. As we moved along towards the dock gates we heard comments from passengers returning to this ship about the difference in size, and their thoughts on how much more it must have cost to be on *'Oriana'*. We said nothing, as by now we believed we had found good value, and secretly wondered how *'Oriana'*s quality could be matched on such a small ship.

The town is about a mile from the dock and you can take a taxi, but we walked to get a little more exercise. The road to the town is bare and only the occasional tree gives any shade during the few minutes walk, but we were prepared with water bottles, hats, and sun cream like the seasoned tourists we felt we had become.

Arriving in the garrison town of Gibraltar we understood just how British it has tried to remain, with true-to-life pubs and many shops with recognisable names. There were policemen in the uniform of home, red post boxes, traditional traffic lights, and English was the predominant language being spoken. I am however probably going to offend some people now with what I saw that day. If so, I apologise.

A high percentage of the population of Gibraltar is British, and they attract the typical shops and stick to the customs of Britain, but they were not the majority of the people I saw that afternoon. Most shops in the main street are there to attract tourists looking for duty-free bargains, but I do not remember anyone in these shops without a Spanish or Asian accent. While walking along the street the same accented English was what I heard, with rarely a conversation that I could consider unaffected by another language, except when it involved other passengers from *'Oriana'* or the Thomson ship.

The love for Gibraltar is immense and its history was vitally important to the success of our armed forces, but the influence of Spanish, African and Asian cultures is

116

gradually watering down the "Britishness" factor, that currently stops the official barriers coming down between there and mainland Spain.

Anyway, enough of my disloyal thoughts, I can say we enjoyed the shops and we bought various keepsakes. The choice is vast, from electronics through gold or jewellery, to traditional Asian clothing and materials. If you want something I truly believe that Main Street Gibraltar will have it. There were moments when we asked for a particular item that was not on display, and if the shopkeeper did not have it, they directed us to another shop *("he is my brother")* where we would be able to get it.

We sat and had an ice-cream while we watched the locals going about their business, and cruise passengers wandering back and forth looking for the cheapest Benson and Hedges or Jack Daniels amongst the many small outlets. Soon the heat was taking its toll and we started the return walk to *'Oriana'*. The sun was no cooler and the exposed road was quite tiring, but some other passengers we saw seemed affected worse than we were. Perhaps they had sampled a little too much lager, or overindulged on fish and chips, but now overloaded with duty free carrier bags they were struggling in the heat. There were also a few who were rather desperate for a toilet, and with half a mile to go, there were no handy trees or shelters to hide their embarrassment.

Before we knew it we were back at the gangplank and the realisation dawned that this was the last time we would be boarding the ship, and our next time on land would be back in Southampton. Back in the cabin we tucked away our purchases quite silently as we both wondered once more if we could cruise again sometime. Well I did anyway!

As *'Oriana'* was set free from Gibraltar there was a party on board, for the passengers to sing and wave their Union Jack flags as a farewell while they drank and enjoyed the evening sunshine. Then as they turned away and walked back to their cabins to prepare for dinner, perhaps the faces showed just a little sadness as they started to come to terms with knowing that the holiday was nearing the end.

That evening we sailed west along the southern coast of Spain with the sun setting ahead of us. We had enjoyed this weather since leaving Lisbon a fortnight ago, and it had been a glorious holiday. It was such a change from our typical British summer breaks. Looking on the bright side, there were still two nights left, so rather than dwelling on the obvious, we made the most of our remaining time on *'Oriana'*. The food was as good as ever, the shows still entertained us and the ship continued to thrill us with her beauty. No doubts remained in our minds; this holiday was the dream we had hoped for.

That evening one of the choices in the restaurant was roast turkey, and there was a fruit crumble on the menu as well.

Were they trying to remind us that we were going home?

The main cabaret entertainment in the theatre that night was Nicky Martyn again (the ship's comedian) and we laughed throughout the act. He included a poem that he (allegedly) had written for our cruise, based on where we had stopped and things that had happened. It captured the spirit of the holiday perfectly and we kept a signed copy of the poem as yet another memento to be treasured.

The theatre troupe rounded the evening off with a tribute to 'Queen' in the Pacific Lounge. Unlike the traditional stage-based productions, this was a more personal, close-to-the-audience show. It was colourful, with dazzling lights, multiple costume changes and much more "rock" based music.

It had been another good day, and after a late night cup of hot chocolate and a sandwich or two in the *Conservatory,* we made our way back to our cabin. Relaxed and arm in arm we smiled and laughed in the way that we had become accustomed to.

Friday 1st September – Going Home

During the night *'Oriana'* turned northwards little by little, and when I woke at odd moments to roll over in bed, perhaps the movement was just slightly more obvious than I had become used to.

As my eyes opened the next morning, and my senses switched on, there were unfamiliar sounds and feelings. Apart from the occasional swell around the crater of Santorini, the sea had been virtually flat since our first day on board, but now the waves had returned and they were hammering on the hull of the ship. 'Oriana' was moving far less predictably and the wall panels were creaking, and previously stable objects now rattled. It was not rough and I did not feel any discomfort, but the difference was obvious.

Our routine didn't change that morning but as we walked along the deck to breakfast, the cooler wind suggested that tee shirts and shorts may not be the most ideal choice of clothing anymore. The water in the pool was moving in opposition to the ship and created waves and a hint of spray as they hit the ends.

I was taking no chances and took one of the little pills supplied by the doctor a fortnight earlier, to avoid any seasickness spoiling my remaining time on board. It made me feel slightly sleepy but unlike having the injection, I was still able to enjoy what the ship had to offer. The entertainment did not alter just because we were on the last lap of the journey, but there seemed to be more things to do inside, rather than out on the decks. The ship was beginning to labour through the angry sea creating a noticeable rise and fall.

Some passengers were still attempting to swim in the pools, but as the day progressed the waves became quite significant, and fewer people took on the challenge. The sun had also lost a lot of its heat as we moved northwards, but it was still warm enough to enjoy.

Although the day followed the same pattern that I had become used to, there was a niggling feeling that the end was in sight, and thoughts were beginning to shift towards the inevitable process of going home. It was not going to spoil the last two days, and most of the passengers went out of their way to soak up the last of the good weather, the food, the entertainment, and all the experiences that *'Oriana'* had to offer. It was if we were ensuring our memories were going to be too full of happy thoughts to stop normal life taking over until the last possible moment.

That night was the final formal dress night for dinner and I put on my crisply laundered shirt, and Debs wore her last posh frock. The meal was as superb as always and we chatted and laughed our way through dinner, but the talk revolved more around what we had done as a review of the holiday, rather than about specific moments. After dinner we enjoyed a cabaret act (Gary Wilmott again) and topped up the alcohol levels in *Andersons*, finishing with a brandy for Debs and a Drambuie and ice for me. Before bed we wandered around the decks with the sea now becoming seriously angry as we approached the Bay of Biscay. The

121

swimming pool had become a boiling pot of water spilling out all over the surrounding deck. There was a net over it to stop any foolish would-be swimmer risking their lives.

Time for bed and as well as a cup of tea and a packet of biscuits, there was another little pill for me. Tomorrow would be the last day and perhaps the smile on my face was not quite as broad as it had been for the last couple of weeks as I slipped into sleep.

Saturday 2nd September - The Final Day

Good Morning and welcome to the Bay of Biscay.

The official description is to "Round Cape Finisterre and set a north-northeasterly course to cross the Bay of Biscay."

We awoke to irregular movement and creaking sounds as *'Oriana'* started an eleven-hour journey across this stretch of water. Biscay is renowned for its ability to upset the stomachs of anyone with a chink of weakness in that part of their anatomy. Hence another little white pill was eagerly sought and dispatched. In reality although I knew the sea was rougher than I had experienced on the first day, I did not feel as badly affected as I had been then. On one hand, there was a strong respect for the sea at that moment, but also a sense of wonder at its beauty and power.

On the way to breakfast, our balance was tested as the ship rose and fell in its attempt to plough a furrow through the angry resistive water. Nevertheless we got to the *Conservatory* and as far as I remember I had a hearty English breakfast as had been my way on most mornings. With the trivialities of eating and washing over it was time to find something to do.

Swimming was out. No water remained in the pools as a precaution against foolhardy cruisers, and also to avoid everyone becoming drenched while passing by the pool.

Sunbathing was out. It was grey, damp, and significantly cooler than we had become accustomed to.

Deck games were also out. In fact warnings were posted on the doors to take care when on the open decks.

I recall that Deb took her customary "keep fit" session, and I took my video camera and tried to capture some form of memory of the sea crashing against *'Oriana'*. The ship created huge waves of foam which rose many metres into the air, followed by a moment of calm as the ship rose up over the next wave, before crashing down once more. I found it mesmerising and actually enjoyable to witness this raw power.

Inside again I took to my book, and completed reading it so that it could be returned to the library. I do not normally enjoy reading for pleasure as my job in training meant many hours of reading for research. During this cruise I regained that pleasure. I only read two books but that was a major achievement compared to normal. One of the books was about Albert Pierrepoint, the renowned hangman, while the other was a biography of Richie Benaud (Australian cricketer). Quite an unusual mixture, but it worked for me.

Deb on the other hand was working her way through the books that she had brought with her, plus a serious number of others from the ship's library. She can curl up with a book and instantly sink into it for what seems an eternity to me. I on the other hand prefer to see a picture rather than to imagine it, and books can only capture my attention for short periods. Staring at the television both visually stimulates my imagination to become a part of the plot, and relaxes my mind from the humdrum world of training.

Without television for the duration of the cruise, I relied on the scenery around me for visual satisfaction, and this cruise had certainly come up trumps. Whether it was the simplicity of the water, the beauty and colours of the landscapes, or awe at the architecture, my mind had been stimulated to a level that it was if I was drunk from this visual drug.

But we had one task to do that was the final reminder that home beckoned.

We had to pack our cases.

It was not difficult, even though we had more to put in now than we brought with us. It was just the realisation that this was one of the final acts of any cruise that passengers have to suffer. Of course it was good to remind ourselves of all the little keepsakes we had bought, and this rekindled memories of the places we had visited. Eventually all but the final necessities, plus changes of clothes for the evening and the next morning, were packed away and the suitcases closed and placed outside the cabin door. We just kept back one case for the clothes we were currently wearing to go in before bedtime, and a holdall each for the rest. Out in the corridor numerous bags were appearing as the afternoon wore on.

The rest of the afternoon passed quietly for both Deb and myself, and it was soon time for our final afternoon drink and individual quiz in the *Lords Tavern*, and then onwards to dinner. As we left the cabin to go to dinner all of our cases were gone and very few remained in the corridors to be collected.

Would we ever see them again?

The last night of the cruise had a different atmosphere from any other we had experienced. For a start the dress code was officially 'casual', but in reality it was a very relaxed casual. There were no denim jeans, or scruffy tops, but certainly people looked more dressed for a night in a pub, compared to their previous attire used for this dress code.

The final dinner was to the same standard as we had become used to, and rounded off with a special treat for our waiters as well as ourselves. We had brought our little brown envelope with the tip for the waiters, just as we had left a similar one on the bed for our cabin steward. I never begrudged them their tips, as the standards of service both in the cabin and the restaurant were exceptional.

Our treat, was for the waiters to present each couple with a bundle of the menus that had been used throughout the cruise. These were not just plain menus, but each one had a cover picture of cruise ships from the past. I am sure that some seasoned cruisers give a polite thank-you, and later dispose of them, but we kept ours along with all the handouts that came our way during the cruise.

Sad? Yes, but we feel they were worth keeping as a wonderful reminder.

126

We exchanged addresses and bade farewell to our dinner table friends, and went back to the cabin to open the curtains (as we always did) and then moved on to the theatre. The last show was themed on a Rio Carnival with lots of samba rhythms, brightly coloured costumes, and tall hats for the girls. The theatre troupe worked hard to entertain us throughout the cruise with rarely a night off.

From there we moved to *Harlequins* to listen to the band, "Natural High", for the last time with a drink or two as we watched the dancers. This was a sad aspect of our past in that we had never learnt to dance a waltz or a quickstep, so our only active contribution was when a Barn Dance or the Gay Gordans came along.

Later, we strolled around the outside decks, and pausing at the stern for a while, we realised that the sea was calming down. *'Oriana'* had rounded the northern end of Biscay at about 7 o'clock that evening, and we were now on the home straight to Southampton. Sadly we returned indoors and took a final nightcap in *Andersons*.

"Your usual, Mr and Mrs Williams?"

During the short time on board we had made our little mark in that bar with the waiter knowing our taste. We accepted his offer and were soon sipping our drinks - a Drambuie for me and a brandy for Deb. We sat back and relaxed as we chatted about the cruise, and although the memories were still fresh and vivid in our minds, they could not take away just a little sadness that we were going home.

127

Bedtime came, and we nibbled our final chocolates before a goodnight cup of tea and a packet of biscuits.

Sunday 3rd September – Southampton

Damn it!

We awoke to discover that the captain had gone the right way and we had arrived in Southampton.

Time was just a little more critical that morning, as we had to vacate the cabin before 8 o'clock. That meant getting to breakfast, returning for a final wash, and getting the last bits and pieces packed away. We went to the *Conservatory* to discover that it was packed out with people who had not normally got out of bed much before 10 o'clock, and who were now cramming a breakfast before their journey home. It was the first time we had struggled to find somewhere to sit for the entire cruise. We only had a light breakfast that day, even though the full choice was available as always. The opportunity was taken to make a couple of bacon rolls to snack on during the journey home.

Back in the cabin we discovered that the steward had already stripped our bed, and whisked away any bits and pieces that we might have naughtily helped ourselves to. We brushed our teeth and packed away washing bits into our holdalls, along with passports, English money, and various documents from the safe. There was a last look around the cabin followed by a sigh as we dropped our keys onto the desk and made our way to the waiting area.

A couple of nights before this we had received our disembarkation tickets, telling us of the expected time that we could be getting off. Just like coming onto the ship, only a few passengers were allowed off at any one time to minimise the congestion whilst searching for the luggage.

It was going to be nearly two hours before we were to get off, so we found a comfy corner in the *Pacific Lounge* to sit and wait. Newspapers were being sold, and a long queue had formed to grab a paper and get up to date with the news.

'Oriana' no longer seemed like the cruise ship we had been on for seventeen days. It seemed more like a hotel lobby, with hundreds of people filling every possible seat with themselves and small luggage items. All the smiles and joviality that we had become accustomed to had gone. The holiday was over.

Deb and I took turns for a final stroll around the ship to break the boredom of waiting. The loading of food and drink for the next cruise had already begun, and I knew that soon passengers for the next cruise would be arriving as we had, and would be watching from the viewing gallery the spectacle of *'Oriana'* preparing for its next adventure.

The time had come, and after a final *Bing Bong* we were called to disembark. Along the corridor, down the staircase to the bottom of the *Atrium* and out through the doors to a non-stop chorus of *"Goodbye, I hope we see you again soon"* from the entertainment staff who were on duty to see us off. Down the gangway we bounced to the quayside and into the terminal building. There was very little time to reflect on much, but even if tears were not showing in our eyes, the sadness of leaving *'Oriana'* was making us well up inside.

Before us stood row upon row of suitcases in deck order waiting to be claimed. The first task was to grab a trolley and make our way to Row C and then to spot our cases. It is amazing how many people have the same colour and style of cases. Eventually all our pieces were found and piled onto the trolley and we made our way to the exit. There was a slight moment of panic as we chose the Green Custom route in case we looked guilty enough to be randomly picked for a search. A small number of people were looking very annoyed as the contents of their cases were spread over the counters. We walked on and out into the next hall to reclaim our car.

At the little booth I handed over the receipt, and our car keys were returned with simple instructions as to where our car was waiting. The trolley was a little overloaded, and the route to the car park involved crossing a road with various slopes, as well as recessed railway lines and pavements, so occasionally we had to stop to recover a bag or to reposition the luggage in a more balanced state. The car was quickly found and the baggage replaced in the boot. We joined the queue of vehicles heading for the exit, and within probably ten minutes of walking off the ship we were back on the road towards Staffordshire.

On the way home we stopped in Abingdon for a snack (the bacon rolls were forgotten) and also to fill up with petrol. Onwards to the M40 and eventually the M6 took us home, and we sat quietly in the car for most of the journey. Very soon we were turning into the drive of our house to unpack, and start the process of returning to normality.

After the initial *"hello"* and *"how are you"* discussion with the children, and the handover of presents, we had a cup of tea and then it was time to start tidying things away.

The next hour consisted of putting any clean clothes away, and turning seventeen days of dirty clothes into piles to take their turn in the washing machine.

Deb worked solidly for two days to get the washing completed.

Piles of keepsakes were created until a suitable place was found for them. Cameras were stored away and their films made ready for developing and printing to bring the memories of the holiday back. Suitcases were returned to the loft, and emergency shopping completed to see us through our immediate needs.

That evening the house seemed so still as we sat and chatted over our experiences. Odd items were picked up with a question such as *"where did we get this*?" that re-ignited a memory. We were still both on fire from the experiences that we had savoured, but we were also sad to think that it was over.

One of the booklets that had been handed out on the last day was a résumé of the cruise, and the facts there gave a very good indication of just how much we had done.

During those 17 days we had sailed 6422.9 nautical miles, visiting seven ports in three different countries (plus Gibraltar) and on two different continents.

It had cost a lot of money, and during the planning there had been many moments of doubt that it was the correct decision.

.

Back to Normal

The next day I returned to work carrying my little bust of Sophocles from Athens and a head full of memories.

That first week was a struggle to come back down from the dream I had been living, and at any slightest chance, I was telling people of the experiences I had had and was boring my colleagues to despair.

At home the photographs came back from the printer and the evenings were filled with looking at them together with my video footage, but much of the time was spent in silence just thinking about *'Oriana'* and the memories.

Days turned to weeks and life returned to normal, but there was always an 'itch' in the background that the experience really had to be more than a one-off, and that for us cruising was the perfect holiday that had to be repeated.

Deb and I thought hard as the days went by, and a realisation dawned on us that we had to find a way of taking further cruises. Thus we made the decision to sell our caravan and the money raised proved sufficient to pay for a cruise the following year. From then on it became our way of life each summer right up to the present day.

Coming up to date

That cruise was 17 years ago, and since then we have had at least one cruise every year. The cruise industry has changed dramatically over that period and what was seen as a luxury holiday for the few, has diversified and become available, and affordable, for the masses. More ships have been introduced, and they are significantly bigger than Oriana. Instead of delighting less than 2000 passengers, these gigantic floating holiday camps cater for upwards of 5000 people at a time.

Ships no longer look like the traditional ocean going liners and instead resemble a floating block of flats. The majority of cabins have balconies, and some even offer cabins with windows facing internally over vast walkways running long lengths of a ship with shops and cafes.

They are vast, and offer real family holiday experiences with an incredible range of entertainment. On the open deck they have climbing walls, flumes, fairground rides, and huge video screens. Eating choices have moved on from the 'formal' dining options of the past. Those formal dining rooms remain, but are becoming less popular with some passengers who don't want to dress up, or be restricted to fixed eating times. There are smaller restaurants and bistro style options offering food from all over the world on demand.

Strangely the increase in cabin choice, entertainment, and food options has not pushed the prices of cruise holidays up. The price of a balcony cabin today is very little more than we paid for an outside cabin in the year

2000. The massive capacity of the ships means more income per cruise, whilst massive improvements in engine and propulsion efficiencies have also kept prices low.

But, something has to change to keep profits high. Other than the main dining rooms, passengers have to pay supplements for the majority of eating choices. Shops and photographers are franchises which have to buy the right to trade on the ships. They have to charge quite ridiculous prices to make money.

Free perks that we enjoyed such as the cabin steward bringing a wake up cup of tea have gone. That steward would have been servicing maybe 9 cabins a day when we first cruised, but now they have to look after closer to 20 cabins in the same time. This is an obvious cost saver, but means cabins simply cannot get the same level of attention.

The number of entertainment crew has reduced, and visiting cabarets are rarely of the same standard as in the past. Of course the theatre team are still wonderful, but regular cruisers have seen the shows too many times to be amazed anymore.

Meals in the dining room are plated, and have lost the wow factor in terms of choice and quality. The traditional chocolates with the coffee are more likely to be a small piece of dry cake, and there are rarely items of fruit at the end of a meal. On the subject of chocolates, the nightly pillow chocolates are now cheap and cheerful, and the cabin biscuits are no longer worth hoarding....or eating.

All though I might sound negative, we still adore cruising and we have remained loyal to P&O. There have been some absolutely wonderful holidays on seven different ships of the fleet. We also experimented with another cruise line (Fred Olsen) which was enjoyable, but not good enough to tempt us away from P&O.

Our trips have mainly been to the Mediterranean, Adriatic and Aegean areas but we have also ventured to the Canaries, Azores, Norwegian Fjords, Baltics, different ports around the British Isles, and even an amazing full three month circumnavigation of the world.

We have hundreds of hours of video footage and thousands of photographs that can help us recall the magic...

...and yes, we still have those original promotional videos that have been transferred to DVDs, and we still watch them over a glass of wine.

Deb has made-up a file for each holiday containing the most memorable photographs plus daily programmes and menus from each cruise. These have pride of place on the bookshelf and have been shown to anyone that has the slightest interest. Looking through them has revealed that we have been on over 25 cruises, with in the region of 400 nights at sea, and we have travelled well over 100,000 nautical miles so far.

Those cruises have allowed us to return to all of the ports from that first adventure, except Santorini.

I still tremble with the expectation of a cruise, and go light-headed as I park up at the terminal in Southampton. The buzz of excitement increases when I board the ship, and this stays with me throughout the holiday. At the end I leave the ship with sadness, but that only lasts as long as it takes to start thinking about, and planning the next one.

That first cruise in the year 2000 was chosen as a "*one-off*" special event, but it turned out to be the start of 17 years, of special events...so far.

Also like that first cruise, our world cruise in 2012 was supposedly planned as a "*once in a lifetime*" retirement present. Well it was so good that our next major voyage is a repeat of that adventure in January 2017.

I constantly look back and sigh as the memories of our cruises flood back. The back of my neck still tingles with affection pride and excitement, when I see pictures of those beautiful ships, and with no doubts about the decision we made, I feel so delighted that this Cornishman went cruising!

September 2016

Other Books by the Author

Around the World without Wings

The author and his wife retired at the end of 2011 and they needed something really special to celebrate this moment.

So on a cold January evening in 2012 they left Southampton on the cruise ship MV Aurora on an adventure that would change their outlook on life, with a circumnavigation of the world lasting over three months.

Travel with them and share their thrills, laughter, and yes a few tears, as they discover so many amazing countries, cultures, and experiences on their journey around the world.

A Cornishman Cruises to Venice

Venice has become one of the author's favourite cities in Europe, and hence is a regular port of call on the couple's summer cruises. As well as the beauty and magic when visiting this Italian gem, the book also explores the nearby historical city of Dubrovnik.

George and Deb always begin and end their cruises at Southampton, so the book spends time talking about the different ports that are also visited on the way to and from the Adriatic.

A Cornishman cruises the Western Mediterranean

The cruise ship adventures of the author and his wife (Deb) have visited many of the wonderful mainland Mediterranean ports of Spain, France and Italy, as well as numerous islands.

This volume of the Cornishman's maritime holidays, concentrates on the Western Mediterranean destinations.

Time for Tea and a Cheese Scone

Retirement at the end of 2011 brought new challenges for George and Deb, as well as the freedom from work.

The author kept a diary of the first year of retirement after over forty years of employment, and this book looks at the winter months as the couple get used to a new way of life.

Would You like Some Plums?

Following on from the first book about their retirement, this book looks at the summer months in 2013.

As the couple enjoy their release from work, they decide to move to a new home.

Along with so many different things that the couple experienced in that six months, the house move becomes a major topic of this book.

You Need a new Hip

Like many thousands of people each year the author was shocked when he was told he needed a new hip. This book shares his experiences leading up to the diagnosis, and then the operation itself plus the first year of recovery.

Hip replacements are very common but George struggled to find out more than the basic facts of what the procedure involved, and certainly very little information existed for the quite lengthy recovery period. To help others that might be waiting for a replacement, or have just had one, this book might help to clear up some of the questions and will hopefully give you confidence for the eventual outcome.

A Cornish Boy Grows Up

This book is a rework of a previous book entitled See 'e 'gen Cornwall. Although much of the material is the same, the emphasis is on the author's early years, and school life until he begins full time employment.

George Williams was born in Cornwall at a time when life was far simpler and slower than children experience today. Holidaymakers come in their thousands to Cornwall each summer, to enjoy the golden beaches, but, many also become fascinated by the County's Myths and Legends. Tiny fishing villages are full of locals speaking in an accent that is both sweet and confusing to a visitor's ear, and stories are recounted of Pirates and Piskies while they eat the famous pasties or cream teas.

The author grew up with his parents and three brothers, and life was full of fun with a small group of friends, but there were also some dark moments and tragedies. The lazy Cornish way of life did little to encourage George to take his education very seriously, and by the time he left in 1968 he had only acquired a handful of qualifications to attract the interest of prospective employers.

In this book the author candidly recounts the first phase of his life, as he makes his way from infant innocence, through painful hormone changes of adolescence, to the realisation that growing up means more than playtime.

He also tries to give a flavour of Cornwall's uniqueness and beauty to those who have never sampled its delights, and attempts to share his love for the County.

Printed in Great Britain
by Amazon